"I used these ideas in class and had a wonderful day with my students."

Thank you so much!! I used these ideas in class and had a wonderful day with my students. As a first Year Relief Teacher I find this site invaluable in helping me become a better and more confident Teacher.

Jess (Take Control of the Noisy Class customer)

* * *

"It is very rewarding to see a teacher apply strategies from Rob's materials, then get excited as they see the 'magic' work."

"The materials have been right on target, students have benefitted as well as teachers. It is very rewarding to see a teacher apply strategies from Rob's materials, then get excited as they see the 'magic' work. Thank you for making my job easier and validating the experience."

Cheryl E. Le Fon (Take Control of the Noisy Class customer)

Attention-Grabbing

Starters & Plenaries for Teachers

99 Outrageously Engaging Activities to Increase Student Participation and Make Learning Fun

Needs-Focused Teaching Resource Book 2

Rob Plevin

http://www.needsfocusedteaching.com

About the Author

Rob Plevin is an ex-deputy head teacher and Special Education Teacher with the practical experience to help teachers in today's toughest classrooms.

No stranger to behaviour management issues, Rob was 'asked to leave' school as a teenager. Despite his rocky route through the education system he managed to follow his dream of becoming a teacher after spending several years working as an outdoor instructor, corporate trainer and youth worker for young people in crisis. Since then he has worked with challenging young people in residential settings, care units and tough schools and was most recently employed as Deputy Head at a PRU for children and teenagers with behaviour problems. He was identified as a key player in the team which turned the unit round from 'Special Measures'.

He now runs needsfocusedteaching.com, is the author of several books and presents training courses internationally for teachers, lecturers, parents and care workers on behaviour management & motivation. His live courses are frequently described as 'unforgettable' and he was rated as an 'outstanding' teacher by the UK's Office for Standards in Education.

Rob's courses and resources feature the Needs-Focused Approach™ – a very effective system for preventing and dealing with behaviour problems in which positive staff/student relationships are given highest priority.

To book Rob for INSET or to enquire about live training please visit the help desk at

www.needsfocusedteaching.com

Introduction

Free bonus materials & printable resources

This book, like the others in this series, is for teachers like you who want to connect and succeed with tough, hard-to-reach students in the shortest possible time. To help you do this, it comes complete with additional bonus material as well as printable resources to accompany the activities explained in the book.

 Wherever you see the **'resource icon'** in this book, head over to our website to get your free resources and accompanying printables,

Please visit:

http://needsfocusedteaching.com/kindle/starters

About the Book

Attention-Grabbing Starters and Plenaries is book #2 in my Needs-Focused Teaching Resource series. This collection of teaching books is my attempt to provide teachers with practical, fast-acting, tried-and-tested strategies and resources that work in today's toughest schools. The novel, quirky ideas and methods form part of my Needs Focused Approach and have been tried and tested with hard-to-reach, reluctant learners of all ages, in more than 40 countries. Over the last 10 years or more they have been found to be highly effective in improving learning, raising achievement, building trusting relationships and creating positive learning environments.

Each book in this series includes a comprehensive suite of bonus materials and printable resources as I want to give you as much support as possible and for you to be delighted with your book purchase. Please be sure to download your bonus resources from my website here:

http://needsfocusedteaching.com/kindle/starters

The Needs Focused Approach

So, what is the Needs Focused Approach and how can it help you? Well, it's based on Abraham Maslow's Hierarchy of Needs theory which suggests that humans share a wide range of emotional and psychological needs – from the need to achieve through the need to contribute, to the need for love and a whole host of others in between.

The Needs-Focused Approach breaks down these psychological needs into just three broad groups to make life easy. Let me explain what the three groups are and why they are so crucially important in terms of both preventing problems, and responding to students who misbehave. The first group of needs falls under the heading 'Empowerment' and includes things like recognition, freedom, autonomy, achievement, contribution, choice and competence. Second is the need for 'Fun' and includes curiosity, interest, growth and learning, adventure, amusement, surprise, variety. Finally, is the need to 'Belong' – to be accepted, valued, appreciated, needed, related to or connected with something beyond oneself.

If you think about it, few of us function well without adequate control, choice, autonomy and freedom in our lives - we need to be empowered. We can't live happy lives without at least some variety, humour, activity or fun. And we feel isolated and alone if we're not valued or appreciated by others or connected to them in some way - we need to belong. When these three needs are NOT being met - when they are missing from our lives - we tend to feel frustrated and unsettled. That's when the problems start.

Consider the following scenario: imagine if you will, a thoroughly boring lesson. You know the type I mean – a teacher handing out worksheet after worksheet, standing at the front of the room, like a shop-window dummy going through the motions.

There's no engaging warm-up activity to grab the students' attention, no variety or choice in terms of lesson tasks or level of challenge, no novelty or intrigue, no humour, no laughter, no sense of discovery, no interaction or movement around the room, no music, no curious props, no energiser, no recognition or praise for efforts made and no attention given to differing learning styles. It's the kind of lesson that makes kids want to get up and walk out.

What usually happens in a lesson like this? You guessed it: students misbehave. It might start with fairly innocent activities such as doodling or passing notes, but left unchecked the activities become increasingly disruptive: getting up and walking around, throwing things, shouting silly comments, dishing abuse to the teacher, not doing work, tapping pencils, refusing to follow instructions, dictating their own terms, using mobile phones etc. What has resulted is the typical behaviour problems arising from frustration and dissatisfaction – from needs that have not been met.

Remember, our psychological needs are crucial to us and must be satisfied – they are a primeval, subconscious thirst which must be quenched and as important to us as water and sunlight are to a plant. If the teacher doesn't provide a means to meet these needs as part of regular day-to-day practice, students will seek satisfaction in less appropriate ways of their own devising. In other words, if you don't give them fun, they'll make their own. If you don't give them a sense of power, they will assert themselves in their own way. And if you don't make them feel valued they will opt out and form trouble-making splinter groups. (Have you ever wondered why 'gangs' are so appealing to young people?)

Throughout this book, I will present ideas and activities which help satisfy these three key needs in order to help you prevent a large proportion of behaviour related problems from ever arising in your classroom. I don't claim that all your problems will be solved but by adopting the strategies and ideas that follow you will definitely see a dramatic reduction in the number of incidents you're currently dealing with on a daily basis. And I guarantee you'll see an improvement in student attitudes and lesson engagement.

The activities in this book will help students feel a sense of belonging – by making them feel part of the classroom community, by strengthening peer relationships and by building positive, mutually respectful student-teacher bonds. They will empower your students by providing them with realistic chances to achieve and experience success, by giving them a degree of autonomy and choice and by ensuring their efforts are recognised and acknowledged. And they will improve motivation in lessons by making lessons more interactive and appealing, more stimulating, more relevant and more fun.

Now, without further ado, let's get started...

Part 1.

The perfect lesson start

It doesn't take much to ensure a lesson fails. In fact, you can do it before the students get through the door. A frown, some harsh words and over-the-top warnings are usually sufficient to send the mood of your typical student plummeting and have them conclude that the next 60 minutes are going to be thoroughly miserable for all concerned.

But let's assume you've worked hard to establish a warm and welcoming tone at the door and the students trudge through to their seats with a reasonably positive outlook – as explained in my classroom management manual 'Take Control of the Noisy Class – From CHAOS to Calm in 15 Seconds'. They sit down full of hope and expectation – eager to discover what you've got planned for them.

"What are we doing today Miss?"

The success of the lesson now depends largely on your starter or opening activity and it could go one of two ways. If you manage to hook them and arouse their natural curiosity about some new concept you have a good chance of leading them into a successful learning experience, cementing your already-positive relationship with them and chalking up another 'win'. On the other hand, if your choice of opener fails to grab them, it is likely you'll spend the next hour doing nothing but sort out problems.

You need a strong opening or starter activity

Remember the saying 'You never get a second chance to make a first impression'? Whoever wrote it was obviously aware of the sheer carnage often created as a result of a poor lesson opener.

If you lose your students in the first 2 minutes you'll spend the next 58 minutes trying to get them back. Lose them half way through the lesson and it's a bit easier to re-focus them but unless you get their attention from the outset, the rest of the lesson is going to be, at best, very difficult.

In this book I'm going to present a variety of strategies and activities to grab the attention of your students and get them involved from the very start of the lesson.

An ineffective way to start a lesson

Before we look at our first engaging starter activity let's look at something which turns your students off at the start of lessons straight away...

...Asking the wrong type of questions

I used to start the majority of my lessons with a question relating to the topic focus. For example, if I was doing a lesson on the circulatory system, my opening question might be...

"How many of you can explain what a blood vessel is?"

A few students would be eager to answer me and their hands would shoot up so I thought I was doing the right thing. I had some participation after all.

But for every hand that went up there were 10 more that didn't. A significant proportion of the students simply weren't taking part. And if they are not taking part, as we well know, they soon start to misbehave.

Let's face it, it was a dull question. No matter how passionately it is delivered that type of question isn't likely to generate much involvement from the group.

Questions like this rely on **volunteers**.

If you rely on 'volunteers' you are immediately switching your attention and lesson focus towards those students who *already want to learn*.

That makes it far too easy for those who aren't motivated to learn to simply sit and watch, perhaps pretending to listen. Why should they bother taking part? They have no reason for doing so. They find the subject dull and they either don't know the answer to the question or don't want to answer. Maybe they are afraid of looking 'swatty' in front of their peers; maybe they don't want to risk the embarrassment of getting it wrong. It's easier just to sit and watch.

If you want to get the non-volunteers involved you've got to make the first few minutes INTERESTING and RELEVANT to them and give them a way of responding which isn't threatening. We need to present an activity which is ENJOYABLE for them so that they WANT to get involved. Here's one way of doing it...

...Ask the RIGHT TYPE of questions and use them as a basis for an ENJOYABLE activity

Let's return to the blood vessel question to illustrate what I mean by the right type of question first of all. If we're going to get these students involved we have to have a question that they can relate to, something that relates to their interests or is at least relevant to their lives and experiences. Why would they even care how blood gets round the body unless I make the question relevant to them?

See if you can spot the difference between the following styles of question:

A) Who can tell me how blood gets round the body?

B) Who knows what a blood vessel is?

C) Can anyone tell me what a blood capillary is?

D) When did you last cut your finger badly?

Here are some more...

A) Give me five differences between Macbeth's character before and after he kills Duncan

B) How does Macbeth change after he kills Duncan?

C) What words would you use to describe Macbeth at the start of the play?

D) When was the last time you did something really terrible that you later regretted?

Can you see why 'D' in both cases would be far more likely to get them listening and switched on? Those questions hook them by giving them opportunity to think about events that are RELEVANT to them or have had a direct effect on them.

OK, that's the type of question that will 'hook' your students, but if we're going to use a question like 'When did you last cut yourself really badly?' as a link to a lesson on the circulatory system, for example, we would obviously need to follow up with further questions.

The complete set of questions you put to them might look something like this:

"When did you last cut your finger badly? How long did it bleed for? How did you stop the bleeding? Do you think it would it have stopped if you had just left it? Where does the blood come from and how does it get to the cut?"

As I'm writing this, I've suddenly become aware that my choice of starter question for my lesson on the circulatory system must seem rather macabre to some people and my question for the Macbeth lesson is equally morbid! My lessons aren't usually focused on gloom, doom and terrible events – it must just be a phase I'm going through!

The problem with any type of question is that if it demands an immediate verbal response, it puts people on the spot which gives them a very good reason to not respond. Clearly, being put 'on the spot' doesn't constitute an ENJOYABLE activity.

There's an easy way round that though. Instead of asking them to respond **verbally**, get them to write their answer/s down – either on a piece of scrap paper or a dry wipe board. And make sure you give enough time for this – about two minutes is reasonable because you want everyone to have at least one response written down. That way you are no longer dependent on volunteers everyone can take part by simply reading what they've written.

There will no doubt still be the odd student who drags his heels but we can encourage participation further by reminding them that their ideas are important and that they will be sharing them with the rest of the group – no exceptions, everyone participates.

Next, we can use these questions as the basis for our ENJOYABLE activity – get them to discuss their answers... with a <u>partner</u>.

Pair work is powerful. It features prominently in my sister book on Cooperative & Active Learning and is as practical for small groups as it is for large classes of 40+. One of the benefits is that students can share ideas in a safe 'bubble' before airing their comments publicly to the rest of the group. Some people find speaking out in a group situation incredibly threatening – particularly when the subject is new to them – so giving them a means of 'testing out' their ideas gently coaxes them into active participation which they may otherwise avoid.

Finally, we can make the transition from this initial discussion about their own experiences to some factual learning about the systems behind these experiences.

Do you see what we've done?

We've picked the RIGHT TYPE of question – a question which relates to them and their experiences and gets them INTERESTED and eager to take part.

We've given them a non-threatening way of responding (writing their responses down).

We've encouraged participation by telling them that they will be sharing their answers but made the sharing process very easy for them as they only have to read what they've written down rather than 'think on the spot'.

We've injected some fun (and further allowed them to 'test' sharing their views and ideas in a safe environment) by getting them to pair up and discuss with their partner.

We've introduced a new concept to the whole class rather than focusing our attention on a handful of volunteers.

We've prevented the problems normally associated with switched-off, bored, uninterested students.

So that's one attention-grabbing way of starting your lessons. Let's now jump into the starter activities...

Starter Activities

'What's in the Bag?'

Number of people: Unlimited

Age group: Any

Materials: Prop related to the lesson content together with a suitable bag or container.

Time: 10 minutes

Overview: A lesson-related prop is hidden in a bag or container. Students must guess what's inside. Younger students may enjoy this as a regular routine ("What's in the bag today?") but older students also enjoy it as an occasional, fun warm up.

Directions:

1. Write on the board 'You have 20 chances to guess what's in the bag'.

2. Explain to students that they can volunteer to ask a question to try and determine what's in the bag. Questions can only be those which have a 'yes' or 'no' answer, ie they can ask "is it blue?" but not "what colour is it?"

3. Write their questions down on the board one at a time to keep track of the total number asked and to avoid repeated questions. Answer them "Yes" or "no" and put a tick or a cross next to the question. (I always like to have two noise effects for right and wrong answers to add to the humorous atmosphere... a kazoo or duck call for wrong answers and a bugle horn or quiz master's bell for right answers. Be sure to carry an even-tempered duck if you choose this route.)

4. Tension mounts once their questions are into double figures as they realise they might not succeed – particularly when you tell them they will get extra homework if they don't get the right answer!

Starter Dice

Number of people: Unlimited

Materials: Question Dice. See template in the resources which accompany this book here:

http://needsfocusedteaching.com/kindle/starters

Time: 10-15 minutes

Overview: Students use a **'Question dice'** to generate and answer questions about the topic.

Directions:

1. Print out the template on card and assemble the die.

2. Write on the board suitable questions to match the prompts on the die such as:

   • How could this topic be useful to you in/outside school?

   • What do you already know about this topic?

   • Who will help you throughout this topic?

   • What activities would you prefer to take part in throughout this topic?

   • Why would it be good to do your best in this topic?

   • What will happen if you don't do your best in this topic?

- Who would be a good person to ask about this topic?

- When have you heard about this topic in the past?

- Where have you seen this topic outside school?

- When will you use the information that you learn?

3. A student comes up to the front, rolls the die and answers the relevant question before choosing the next student to take their place.

Generic Starter 3:

'Fish Bowl'

Number of people: Unlimited

Age group: Older students (11-18)

Materials: None required although students may wish to use clip boards to take notes

Time: 10 minutes

Overview: An active starter used at the start of a unit to discover what students already know about a subject and to create 'buy-in' by introducing the work in an enjoyable, interactive way. This activity can also be used very effectively as a plenary activity.

Directions:

1. Divide the class into two even groups.

2. Ask Group 1 to form a circle in the center of the room facing outwards towards the walls.

3. Ask Group 2 to form a circle around the outside of Group 1 facing inwards.

4. Both groups should then move so that they are facing someone from the opposite circle.

5. Tell students you will start a two-minute timer and partners will discuss everything they know, together with everything they would like to know, about this new subject.

6. Sound a horn to signify the end of the two minutes and then ask everyone in Group 2 to move two places to the right and stand opposite their new partner.

7. Repeat step 5.

8. At the end ask students to feed back the things they know and the things they want to know.

Generic Starter 4:

Snowball

Number of people: Unlimited

Materials: None

Time: 5 minutes

Overview: A fun, active (if a little 'frenzied') way to generate student questions about a new topic and provide the teacher with valuable feedback.

Directions:

1. Issue students with scraps of paper and felt tip pens.

2. Ask them to write down (clearly) the following three pieces of information:

   I. Something they already know about the new topic

   II. Something they want to know about the new topic

III.An activity they would like to have included in future lessons

3. Give them a minute or two to write down the information and then tell them to screw up their pieces of paper into a ball.

4. On the command 'SNOWBALL' have the students throw their balls of paper at each other across the room.

5. Students pick up someone else's ball of paper, unwrap it and read the three sentences. If they agree with any of the statements they put a large tick next to the statement before passing the paper on to their neighbour.

6. The idea is to get students to read as many pieces of paper as they can and add ticks to those they empathise with. After five or six minutes stop the activity and get students to pass all the papers to the front of the room for collection. The statements with most ticks are those to focus on.

Generic Starter 5:

Group Hang Man

Number of people: Unlimited

Materials: None

Time: 5-10 minutes

Overview: This game needs little explanation but despite being well-known and perhaps overlooked, its versatility for classroom should not be forgotten. It can be used for absolutely any subject and is surprisingly well received by most groups.

Directions:

1. Split the class into teams (competition is a good motivator for games which aren't dependent on academic ability, but be wary of

setting up competitions in class which are – doing so will often discourage the very students you are trying to involve).

2. Draw a line down the middle of the board and write the team names, one on each side. Draw a picture of an agreed version of 'Hang Man' on the board to illustrate exactly what the finished product will look like and prevent objections such as "We haven't lost! What about eyes? You haven't drawn eyes in yet!"

3. Draw the appropriate number of spaces on the board for the key word you want them to guess and offer each team in turn the chance to guess a letter in the word. If a missing letter is found, they get another go. If the letter they pick is not in the list, the other team takes a turn and the process is repeated until either the word is found or 'Hang Man' is achieved.

Variation:

Issue each student with a list of 40-50 keywords relating to the topic or subject on entry to the room. For obvious reasons, those with a similar number of letters will work best for this exercise. Red herrings and non-related words can also be on the list to pad it out.

Teacher writes spaces on the board relating to a word on the list and students work out which it is. When a student gets the right answer, he/she takes a turn with a new word from the list.

Generic Starter 6:

Question Dominoes

Number of people: Small groups up to 30 maximum.

Materials: Set of pre-written Domino Question Cards

See template in your Resource section here:

http://needsfocusedteaching.com/kindle/starters

Although considerable time is required to make up each set of domino cards, they are a useful resource and well worth the effort - they can be used several times throughout a unit of study as a reinforcement exercise.

Time: 10-15 minutes (depending on the desired number of rounds).

Overview: A twist on the traditional game of dominoes. All students are involved in a linked question/answer activity which can also be used as a plenary activity.

Directions:

1. Prepare a set of domino cards using the template in the resources section. There should ideally be enough cards for each student to have three or four cards.

2. Each card consists of a question statement on one end and an answer on the other. One of the cards is the starting card and has 'FIRST QUESTION' written on it.

3. The student with the starting card asks the question on the card so that all members of the group can hear. The student with the matching answer reads out the answer and then reads out the question from the other end of his/her domino.

In the following example, with a class of just three students, Student A starts by reading the question '2 + 2' which Student B would answer before asking the question '78 + 11' and so on.

NOTE:

This exercise can be differentiated very effectively by issuing answer cards for easier questions to less able students.

Generic Starter 7:

Codename: 'Objective'

Number of people: Unlimited

Materials: Pen, paper and envelope containing 'secret code key' and keyword list for each student

Time: 5-10 minutes

Overview: A creative-thinking starter which can be adapted to suit most subjects and topics.

Directions:

1. Develop a 'secret code alphabet' consisting of a symbol or image for each letter of the alphabet (example below). Give each student a copy, together with a list of keywords about the lesson, in an envelope (labeled 'SPY KIT') as they enter the room.

2. Write a message on the board relating to the lesson using symbols from your coded alphabet e.g. 'Today you will learn about ......'

3. Ask students to decode the message and write their keyword list in a coded form.

4. At the end of the lesson ask students to write a message in code about what they learned.

5. Students can trade papers to decode each other's messages.

Generic Starter 8:

Taboo

Number of people: Unlimited

Materials: Keyword cards

Time: 10-15 minutes

Overview: A fun starter which can be adapted to suit most subjects and topics. Always sure to generate some laughs, this activity also promotes creative thinking and presentation skills.

Directions:

1. Students work individually.

2. One student is selected to come to the front as 'teacher' and is given a card with a keyword written on it. The 'teacher' is given two minutes to describe the word on the card without actually saying the word.

3. When a student guesses the keyword correctly he/she swaps places with the first student and is given a new keyword card.

4. If the keyword isn't guessed within the two minute period, the 'teacher' picks another student to become 'teacher' and the game is repeated with another keyword.

Generic Starter 9:

'KWL'

Number of people: Unlimited

Age group: Any

Materials: Paper and pencils

Time: 10-20 minutes

Overview: A simple starter which can be used to introduce any new piece of material or unit of work

Directions:

1. Write a three-column table on the board or chart paper.

2. Write the letters K, W, L at the top of each column (one per column).

3. Introduce the new topic. (e.g. "Today we are going to start studying mammals.")

4. Ask the students what they already know about mammals.

5. Write their responses in the K (**K**now) column.

6. Once the students have imparted all their knowledge on the topic, ask them if they have any questions about mammals, or if there is anything they would like to learn about mammals.

7. Write down their answers in the W (**W**ant to Know) column.

8. At the end of the lesson, return to the chart to fill in the L (Learned) column about what they have learned.

Generic Starter 10:

Line Up!

Number of people: Unlimited

Materials: Suitable 'content cards' (see below)

Time: 10 minutes

Overview: A very active starter which can be adapted to suit most subjects and topics. It can also be used as a 'getting to know you' type activity.

Directions:

1. The group is told to line up according to the criteria given (see below).

2. An element of challenge can be added to the activity - see if they can lower the amount of time it takes when they repeat it.

Variations-Content Areas

- For **Maths**, give each student an equation and ask them to line up according to their answer (smallest to biggest numbers)

- For **History**, give each student an event that occurred during the study period and ask them to line up in chronological order

- For **Science**, give each student an animal and ask them to form lines showing a food chain

- For **English**, you can hand each student a word. Students need to form 4 lines: articles, adjectives, prepositions, adverbs. Then each line must put itself in alphabetical order.

Generic Starter 11:

Word Jumble

Number of people: Unlimited.

Materials: Word Jumble PowerPoint presentation/Interactive Whiteboard game template in your Resource area here:

http://needsfocusedteaching.com/kindle/starters

Some time is required to pre-set the template with jumbled words and clues.

Time: 5-10 minutes (depending on the desired number of rounds).

Overview: A quick interactive team game where key words have to be unscrambled.

Directions:

1. Prepare the game template by inputting scrambled words and appropriate clues. A maximum of twenty words would be sufficient for any single game.

2. Divide the group into teams. Each group decides on a team name and these are written up on a score board.

3. The game is started by showing a jumbled word together with a clue. The first student to guess the correct word wins a point for his/her team.

4. The game is repeated until all the words have been guessed.

Generic Starter 12:

Dictionary Race

Number of people: Unlimited.

Materials: Dictionaries – one for each pair of students (same type/ edition required – don't give the Shorter Oxford to one team and a Pocket Collins to another!); pad of large post-it notes; pen for each learning pair.

Time: approx. 10 minutes.

Overview: Learning partners race to find definitions of key words using a dictionary. An active, fun starter which reinforces a vital skill and has learners engaged with the lesson topic straight away.

Directions:

1. Teacher decides on a list of four or five keywords and makes sure they are in the dictionary with clear definitions.

2. Students are assigned to learning partners. Learning partners are given two minutes to think of a team name and are told to write this team name at the top of the first five notes on their pads, for easy identification.

3. The chosen keywords are displayed on the board as column headings in a table. Sufficient space is required under each keyword for roughly twenty post-it notes, depending on the size of the group – each learning pair will be posting a note under each keyword.

4. A timer is put on display and a hooter (because we love them) signals the start of the race. One student from each learning pair finds the keyword in the dictionary and the other partner writes the definition on a post-it note. The first partner then sticks the definition on the board under the appropriate keyword.

Note:

I hate to mention the dreaded words 'Health & Safety' as they have been the death knell for too many fun activities. However, it may be prudent to insist that students aren't allowed to run in the classroom during this game (unless of course they wear helmets, eye goggles and protective clothing, and you coat all furniture in bubble wrap).

Anagrams

Number of people: Unlit dime.

Materials: None essentially required although mini-whiteboards add an element of interaction to the game.

Time: 5-10 minutes.

Overview: A very quick and easy-to-set-up 'settling starter'. Students can work individually or in pairs to unravel keywords and phrases relevant to the lesson topic.

Directions:

1. Decide on a number of keywords and phrases and write them on the board in a scrambled format.

2. Given students a set time in which to decipher the letters and write down the answers.

3. When the time is up go through each puzzle in turn and ask students to write down their answer on their mini whiteboards and hold them up.

Early finishers could make up their own anagrams.

<u>**Here are a few to inspire creativity:**</u>

The meaning of life = *The fine game of nil*

Eleven plus two = *Twelve plus one*

Dame Agatha Christie = *I am a right death case*

Desperation = *A Rope Ends It*

The Morse Code = *Here Come Dots*

Dormitory = *Dirty Room*

The Earthquakes = *That queer shake*

Slot Machines = *Cash lost in 'em*

Snooze Alarms = *Alas, No More Z's*

The Public Art Galleries = *Large Picture Halls, I Bet*

That's One Small Step for a Man, One Giant Leap for Mankind =

Thin man ran; makes a large stride, left planet, pins flag on moon. On to Mars!

Generic Starter 14:

What's In My Brain?

Number of people: Unlimited.

Materials: **'Brain'** template in your Resource area here:

http://needsfocusedteaching.com/kindle/starters

Time: 5 minutes.

Overview: A very quick 'settling starter'. Students work individually, reflecting on their current knowledge about a given topic. A good activity to highlight the importance of learning – particularly when introducing a topic which is completely new to them.

Directions:

1. Students are given the 'Brain' template and told to fill in everything they know about the lesson topic.

2. Their ideas are fed back to the group and discussed as a starting point or entry level for the new topic.

Generic Starter 15:

Interactive Team Word Search

Number of people: Unlimited.

Materials: Word Search PowerPoint presentation/Interactive Whiteboard game template in your Resource area here:

http://needsfocusedteaching.com/kindle/starters

Some time is required to pre-set the template with hidden words.

Time: 10-15 minutes (depending on the desired number of rounds).

Overview: Word searches may be 'old hat' but the interactive version, when played in teams, is an engaging cooperative task and a great team-builder.

Directions:

1. Prepare the game template by inputting hidden words and appropriate clues. A maximum of twenty words would be sufficient for any single game.

2. Students form teams or pairs to find the hidden key words. Students should be encouraged to think about how they can best facilitate this task in terms of working as a team – most will quickly catch on the idea of assigning responsibilities (eg, one person looks for diagonal words while another looks for horizontal words).

3. A hooter signals the start of the game and a timer should, ideally, be displayed.

Generic Starter 16:

Traffic Light Starter

Number of people: Groups up to 35.

Materials: 'Traffic Lights' template in your Resource area here:

http://needsfocusedteaching.com/kindle/starters

key points/sentences relating to the previous lesson topic cut into strips and placed in an envelope.

Time: 10-15 minutes.

Overview: Pairs of students are given an envelope containing key points or sentences relating either to the previous lesson's content or new content, together with a 'traffic light' template sheet. This is good exercise for assessing student knowledge prior to a new unit of study.

Directions:

1. Split class into learning partners.

2. Issue envelopes containing strips of key points/subject facts and 'Traffic Lights' template sheets.

3. Students arrange the strips on the Traffic Lights sheet according to their understanding of the statement.

4. Students set themselves a target to improve their knowledge from Red or Amber by the end of the lesson.

Generic Starter 17:

Corners

Number of people: Groups up to 35.

Materials: None required.

Time: 10-15 minutes.

Overview: Students answer questions by moving to an appropriate corner of the room. A very active starter which gets students thinking on their feet.

Directions:

1. Each corner of the room is labeled A, B, C or D.

2. A question is written on the board or shown on a Power Point with four possible answers – A, B, C, D.

3. Students decide which is the correct answer and move to the corresponding corner of the room.

4. Students who get the answer wrong must sit down.

5. The winner is the last student standing.

Note:

Competition is often a great motivator but it can also ostracise less able students if the competition is academically based. For that reason competition between individuals should ideally be limited to non-academic topics. In the game above, adding occasional non-academic questions to the mix will make sure everyone has a chance of progressing through to later stages. Alternatively, the game could be played in learning pairs with each pair consisting of a high ability student teamed with a low ability partner.

Generic Starter 18:

Shark

Number of people: Groups up to 35.

Materials: None required.

Time: 10-15 minutes.

Overview: An active/kinaesthetic version of 'Hangman'.

Directions:

1. A volunteer from the class chooses to be the 'shark bait'.

2. A line is drawn on the floor (the edge of a carpet could just as easily be used) to represent the edge of a cliff above shark-infested waters. The volunteer stands five or six steps away from the 'cliff edge'.

3. The teacher draws the appropriate number of spaces on the board to represent a key word/subject related fact.

4. Students take turns to call out letters and for each letter which isn't present in the key word, the 'shark bait' takes a step closer to the cliff edge.

Active Noughts and Crosses

Number of people: Groups up to 35.

Materials: None required.

Time: 10-15 minutes.

Overview: An active/kinaesthetic version of **'Noughts and Crosses'.**

Directions:

1. Split the class into two teams

2. Draw a noughts and crosses grid on the board

3. A team leader for each team is selected and comes to the board.

4. The teacher asks questions relating to the subject topic.

5. Team members raise their hands to answer the questions, the first hand up getting to give an answer. If they answer the question correctly, their team leader puts their mark on the grid. If they get the answer wrong, play is passed to the other team.

6. Anyone who cheats by shouting the answer out loses the game for their team.

Note:

Games are a great way to reinforce class rules. In this game students are being reminded that they must raise their hands in order to answer a question and that shouting out is not tolerated. Students respond much more positively to rules which are reinforced in this manner as opposed to being 'nagged'.

Constantinople

Number of people: Groups up to 35.

Materials: None required.

Time: 5 minutes.

Overview: A 'quick-to-set-up' game which settles students down and gets them thinking about the lesson topic.

Directions:

1. Write a word on the board related to the subject or lesson content. The longer the word the better.

2. Students are given five minutes to write down as many words as they can think of using the letters in the main word. They are only allowed to use each letter once and they are given bonus points for any words which are related to the topic/subject.

Odd One Out

Number of people: Groups up to 35.

Materials: None required but some thought needs to go into the groups of words chosen.

Time: 5 minutes.

Overview: Triplets of subject-related keywords are written on the board. These could be issued to students on entry to the classroom if this activity is to be used as a 'settling starter'. Students must identify the 'odd one out'.

Directions:

1. Write four or five triplets of keywords on the board, eg:

- farming, drilling for oil, hairdressing

- Pacific, Atlantic, Asia

- hospital, block of flats, cinema

2. Students must identify the odd one out and give a reason for their choice. There is no 'right' or 'wrong' in this exercise – as long as students can give explanations which are logical and/or convincingly explained, their answer should be acceptable. The idea is to develop thinking and communication skills.

Generic Starter 22:

A to Z

Number of people: Groups up to 35.

Materials: None required but some thought needs to go into the groups of words chosen.

Time: 5 minutes.

Overview: A very quick and easy to set up starter which can be extended to a group quiz or competition. The activity can be used for broad topics (French/science etc. or more specific areas such as 'Around town' or 'Acids and Alkalis'.

Directions:

1. Students are given a piece of paper each (one per team if playing in groups) and write down the letters of the alphabet down the side.

2. The lesson topic is written on the board and the students have to think of words related the topic beginning with the letters of the alphabet.

Variation:

Students are allowed to produce 'acrostics' where the letters appear anywhere with the words they think of...

nu**M**ber

r**A**tio

frac**T**ion

pie c**H**art

isoscele**S** triangle

Generic Starter 23:

Brain Gym®

Number of people: Groups up to 35.

Materials: None required but some background music can help.

Time: 5 minutes.

Overview: Brain Gym was developed by Paul Dennison, PhD, creator of Educational Kinesiology. He came to understand how the body was involved in all learning, whatever the subject or area, and a potential source of enhancement for learning skills. In his Valley Remedial Learning Centres, Dr Dennison saw hundreds of adult and child clients and over 25 years evolved a programme that would address this physical component of learning. The programme was known as Educational Kinesiology and part of this programme became the group of body-based movement tools that he named "Brain Gym®".

The reported effects of Brain Gym:

Although Dr Dennison initially used Brain Gym® to help learning, he soon discovered that skills other than academic learning could benefit. These are some of the positive effects commonly fed back by those who use Brain Gym® and those who observe the results, both in the classroom and for personal learning:

Education: improved focus, concentration, calm, memory, listening, speech and language, motivation, self-confidence in approaching new tasks and general learning skills across the subject range.

Social and personal wellbeing: enhanced stress management, communication skills, social skills, ability to plan and take action.

Physical skills: improved co-ordination (gross and fine motor), balance, hand-eye co-ordination, sport and general movement skills.

For more information on Brain Gym® and how to use it as an effective starter activity visit:

http://www.braingym.org.uk/

Generic Starter 24:

Concentration Slide

Number of people: Groups up to 35.

Materials: Concentration slide in your Resource area here:

http://needsfocusedteaching.com/kindle/starters

Time: 3 minutes.

Overview: This is a quick 'settling starter activity' to calm down an unsettled group – or it can be used as a fill-in/brain break.

Instructions:

Put the **'concentration slide'** on the whiteboard and start a timer. Students are given twenty seconds to find as many 'e's/'x's/'3's etc as they can. Numbers/letters can be changed easily.

Generic Starter 25:

Rip-Off Bingo

Number of people: Groups up to 35.

Materials: Narrow ribbons of paper A4 paper cut into lengths down the long side approx. 2cm wide for each student. A list of subject key words displayed on the board.

Time: 5-10 minutes.

Overview: This is a slightly more active variation of bingo.

Instructions:

1. 20-25 subject-based key words are written up on the board.

2. Each student is given a narrow strip of paper which they are told to fold in half three times so as to give eight boxes.

3. Students choose eight words from the selection on the board and write one word into each box on their strip of paper.

4. The teacher calls out words from the list randomly and students 'rip' the word off their paper strip – (as long as the called word is at one end of their strip).

5. The first student to rip their final two words apart and have their final word called is the winner.

Generic Starter 26:

Articulate

Number of people: Groups up to 35.

Materials: Envelopes containing keywords and phrases, a timer

Time: 5-10 minutes.

Overview: A fun activity in which team members are required to describe words to the rest of their team so that they can guess the word. Good for practicing subject-specific terminology and for revising whole topics.

Instructions:

1. Students are arranged in groups of three or four and each group is given an envelope containing 25 words and phrases. Each team nominates one person to be their 'caller'. Teams are allocated a number corresponding to the order in which they will take their turn.

2. A timer is started and the caller from the first team takes a word from their envelope and describes the word to their team mates without saying the actual word. For example, if the student picks 'Stanley Yelnats' (one of the characters from the novel 'Holes') they would describe the character of Stanley (just mentioning the obvious fact that his name is a palindrome would probably suffice in this case).

3. The team is given two minutes to guess as many words from their envelope as possible. They get one point for each word they guess and lose a point if they mention the actual word.

NB// The game is more fun if additional random words are added to the envelope ie. NOT subject related.

Generic Starter 27:

Sentence Builders

Tangible props are a 'never-fail' attention-grabber and it's surprising how much intrigue can be built up with nothing more expensive or creative than an envelope with 'Mission Instructions' written on it. We all love to receive an envelope and guess at its contents which makes this humble piece of stationery the ideal delivery boy for a host of quick activities. Here are five variations on the same theme – give them an envelope with stuff in it and they'll be intrigued enough to at least open it and have a go.

Number of people: Any.

Materials: Pre-written sentence cards in 'mission' envelopes.

Time: 15-20 minutes.

Overview: Students work together in teams during this activity to build sentences based on the lesson topic.

This starter is the type of activity that students can just 'get on with'. It is the perfect settling starter to use when you have to catch up, follow up or deal with individuals who require your full attention - this activity will occupy the rest of the class while you do so. The fact that the task is completed in teams means all students are actively involved.

Directions:

1. Draw up a list of around twelve sentences centered on the lesson topic. Ideally, sentences should contain no more than ten words and the twelve sentences should vary in length and difficulty. Number each sentence and then write each word from each sentence in turn on a separate piece of card. The word cards for each sentence are then placed in an envelope with the sentence number written on the outside; ie, if sentence '1' consists of nine words, envelope '1' will contain those nine words on nine separate cards.

2. Students form groups of three or four and are each given a sheet of paper with the numbers 1 to 12 (or however many sentence envelopes there are) written down the left hand side.

3. The envelopes are placed on a table at the front of the room and one member from each team takes any one envelope back to their team mates. As a group, each team sequences the sentence cards and each team member writes the complete sentence on their sheets next to the relevant number.

4. One person in the team is nominated as 'counter' and counts the sentence cards back into the envelope before replacing it on the front table and taking another envelope. This is repeated until the teams have completed all the sentences.

Generic Starter 28:

Spot the (deliberate) misteak!

Number of people: Any.

Materials: Pre-written cards or pictures sealed in envelopes.

Time: 15-20 minutes.

Overview: This activity can be adapted for any curriculum area. Mistake cards could be sentences which don't make sense, a paragraph with faults in it, a recipe with steps missing and wrong quantities, a sample of a student's work full of errors, a picture with key parts omitted/blanked out, MP's expenses claim etc.

Directions:

1. Arrange ten to twelve envelopes with a selection of 'mistakes' – one sample in each envelope. Number the envelopes 1 to 12.

2. Students form groups of three or four and are each given a sheet of paper with the numbers one to twelve (or however many envelopes there are) written down the left hand side.

3. The envelopes are placed on a table at the front of the room and one member from each team takes any one envelope back to their team mates. As a group, each team finds the mistakes and each team member writes the answers on their sheets next to the relevant number.

4. One person in the team is nominated as 'counter' and counts the mistake cards back into the envelope before replacing it on the front table and taking another envelope. This is repeated until the teams have completed all the envelopes.

Generic Starter 29:

That's an order

Number of people: Any.

Materials: Pre-written cards or pictures sealed in envelopes.

Time: 15-20 minutes.

Overview: This activity can be adapted for any curriculum area. For history it could be a series of dates/events to put in the correct order on a time line; for English it could be a range of adjectives to arrange in order of suitability; for geography it could be a sequence of geological processes, for science it could be a range of pictures which must be put in order to illustrate a scientific procedure etc.

Directions:

1. Arrange ten to twelve envelopes with a selection of statements, words or pictures which need to be arranged in order– one sequence in each envelope. Number the envelopes 1 to 10/12.

2. Students form groups of three or four and are each given a sheet of paper with the numbers 1 to 12 (or however many envelopes there are) written down the left hand side.

3. The envelopes are placed on a table at the front of the room and one member from each team takes any one envelope back to their team mates. As a group, each team puts the statements/pictures in order and each team member writes the answers on their sheets next to the relevant number.

4. One person in the team is nominated as 'counter' and counts the cards back into the envelope before replacing it on the front table and taking another envelope. This is repeated until the teams have completed all the envelopes.

Generic Starter 30:

True or False

Number of people: Any.

Materials: Pre-written True/False statements cards or pictures sealed in envelopes.

Time: 15-20 minutes.

Overview: This activity can be adapted for any curriculum area.

Directions:

1. Arrange ten to twelve envelopes containing two or three statements each.

2. Students form groups of three or four and are each given a sheet of paper with the numbers 1 to 12 (or however many envelopes there are) written down the left hand side.

3. The envelopes are placed on a table at the front of the room and one member from each team takes any one envelope back to their team mates. As a group, each team decides if the statements are true or false and each team member writes the answers on their sheets next to the relevant number.

4. One person in the team is nominated as 'counter' and counts the cards back into the envelope before replacing it on the front table and taking another envelope. This is repeated until the teams have completed all the envelopes.

Generic Starter 31:

Scavenger Hunt

Number of people: Any.

Materials: Clue cards sealed in... ? You guessed it... an envelope.

Time: 15-20 minutes.

Overview: This activity can be adapted for any curriculum area and is tremendous fun. It is also another 'set 'em and forget 'em' type of activity during which the students effectively become self-watering plants. In diverse teams, where peer support naturally occurs, they work to solve the clues, find facts and collate information. Clues can be solved by gathering information online, from offline resources or from a mixture of the two.

The more time you spend setting this up, and the more creative you are with your clues, the more enjoyment your students will get. The only problem with this activity is that your students will want to do it again and again.

Directions:

1. Teacher identifies websites and offline resources such as books, wall displays, relevant experts, newspaper articles etc. together with one specific fact/answer relevant to each source. Questions are constructed for each fact and written on a question/clue sheet.

An extra interactive dimension can be brought into the scavenger hunt by planting some clues around school rather than merely listing them as questions on the question/clue sheet. Budding Sherlocks will be led to find this clue as a result of solving the preceding clue.

For example:

(On the question sheet):

1. In the library on the wall there is a leaflet from the Vegan Society. Write three sentences from the leaflet which suggest dairy farming is cruel.

You will find your next clue under the table directly underneath the leaflet.

Generic Starter 32:

Jumbled Quotes and Phrases

Number of people: Any number.

Materials: 'Jumbled Quotes and Phrases' game in your resource area here:

http://needsfocusedteaching.com/kindle/starters

Time: 10 - 15 minutes.

Overview: A very quick and easy to set up starter or fill-in which can easily be adapted to lesson content by changing the phrases in the game template slides. Students have to unscramble the words to find the hidden motivational phrase. The sample phrases/quotes in the download are suitable for use as discussion starters.

Directions:

1. The game is best played in teams of three-five.

2. Load the Power Point presentation – teams race to unscramble the phrase on each slide and write them down.

3. Phrases are discussed in turn.

Generic Starter 33:

Sit Down

Number of people: Class of approx. 30-35 is optimum.

Materials: none required.

Time: 10 - 15 minutes.

Overview: All students are involved in this keyword-based game where one student tries to catch out the rest of the class. The topic can be curriculum-based although off-topic subjects can be used to create a fun fill-in or energiser.

Directions:

1. A topic is chosen and all students are asked to individually write down a keyword to do with the topic.

2. Everyone stands up and one student (the 'caller') is picked to come to the front and name as many key words to do with the topic as they can in one minute.

3. When a word is called which another student has written, this student must sit down.

4. The object is for the 'caller' to get all the other students to sit down and for the other students to try and think of key words which are relevant to the topic yet sufficiently uncommon so as to avoid being chosen.

The score for each 'caller' is recorded with the winner being the one who can get most people to sit down.

Variation:

Play in teams of four where each team must think up four key words between them – each word being a 'life'. The 'caller' team also create a list of words between them.

"Do you know what it is yet?"

Number of people: Class of approx. 30-35 is optimum.

Materials: Pre-written clue sheets.

Time: 10 - 15 minutes.

Overview: All students are involved in a fun quiz where progressively easier clues are given – either in words or pictures. Teams score points depending on how quick they get the answers.

Directions:

1. Students are arranged in teams of four.

2. The teacher reads out five clues, one at a time, which get progressively easier. Team members have chance to discuss the answer after each clue before writing their answer on paper/a whiteboard and holding it in the air. If the team holds an answer up which is wrong, they are out of the game for that particular question.

3. If a team guesses the correct answer after the first clue they receive 10 points, with subsequent clues dropping in value by 2 points.

Example:

10 points This planet is approximately 856 million miles from the sun.

8 points The diameter of this planet is about 75,000 miles.

6 points This planet is composed mainly of hydrogen gas.

<u>4 points</u> It has more than 30 moons, the largest of which it called Titan.

<u>2 points</u> It has rings made of rock and ice.

4. For fun quizzes like this which require quick-fire answers, you can inject even more fun by giving each team a buzzer to help create the 'quiz-show' atmosphere and you can do this easily and cheaply by having the students create their own. Each team can be offered a choice of animal card and the noise of the animal they pick is their 'buzzer'.

e.g. the 'cow team' will 'moo', the 'donkey team' will 'hee-haw', and the 'three-toed sloth team' will probably want to play something else.

See 'Animal Team Cards' in your Resource area here:

http://needsfocusedteaching.com/kindle/starters

Variation:

Give clues in pictures by either drawing parts of a picture or 'uncovering' a section at a time of a complete picture in a PowerPoint slide.

Note:

Fun games and quizzes like this are wonderful for teaching good behaviour and reinforcing classroom rules. If your classroom rules include 'no shouting out', 'put up your hand to speak' and 'no interrupting', the game provides an ideal vehicle to remind students of these rules in a fun way. i.e. the team loses a point if a team member shouts out an answer or talks over the teacher. Students respond much more positively when they actually experience the benefits of our rules like this rather than hearing us constantly nag them.

Generic Starter 35:

Freeze Frame

Number of people: Class of approx. 30-35 is optimum.

Materials: Photos can be used but not completely necessary.

Time: 10 - 15 minutes.

Overview: All students are involved in production of a 'tableau' to interpret or illustrate a key point. This can be adapted to suit any area of the curriculum – a process in science, an event in history, a social issue, a scene from a story etc. Most students love to role play in groups.

Directions:

1. Students are arranged in groups of four.

2. Each group is given a card with the topic they must illustrate.

3. Groups are given five minutes preparation time and are then asked to 'show back' their 'freeze frames' to the rest of the group.

4. (Phase II) Groups are asked to think about 'what happens next' and move into a 'follow-on' scene. Members of the audience can then volunteer to join in the tableau, adding another dimension if they see fit.

Example:

Lesson: PSHCE.

Topic: 'Bullying'.

Students are instructed to illustrate a bullying scene. Key roles include: Bully/ies, victim and bystanders. Students are asked to 'freeze frame' a typical bullying scene, with bystanders playing a passive role. The scene will vary depending on the location the students choose, the bully:victim:bystander ratio they opt for and the type of bullying they choose to depict.

At phase II, the scene has moved on and the students could be asked to illustrate how the bystanders could get involved to resolve the situation.

During the showback the class would be asked to think about how each individual portrayed is actually feeling – "What might be going through the bystander's mind at this point?"

Generic Starter 36:

Thinking Hats®

Number of people: Any.

Materials: A set of coloured paper hats would be good.

Time: 10 - 15 minutes.

Overview: Students work in pairs or groups using De Bono's 'Six Thinking Hats®'system to fully explore a topic, stimulate group discussion and encourage individual thinking. This tool can be applied to any area of the curriculum using a variety of source materials such as texts, photos, websites, drawings, thoughts/opinions etc.

The coloured hats are used as metaphors for six different states or ways of thinking and by providing students with coloured paper hats, the act of putting a different hat on can symbolise switching to a new thinking state:

- Questions (White) - considering purely what information is available, what are the facts? **("What information do I have?")**

- Emotions (Red) - instinctive gut reaction or statements of emotional feeling (but not any justification). **("What is my gut reaction?")**

- Bad points judgement **(Black)** - logic applied to identifying flaws or barriers, seeking mismatch. **("What don't I like about this?")**

- Good points judgement   - logic applied to identifying benefits, seeking harmony **("What do I like about this?")**

- Creativity (Green) - statements of provocation and investigation, seeing where a thought goes. **("What else?")**

- Thinking (Blue) - thinking about thinking. **("What have I discovered?")**

Directions:

1. Students work in pairs or groups.

2. Each pair or group is given a topic/source materials/item etc on which to apply the Thinking Hats® system.

3. Students can records their ideas on sugar paper – as large mind maps – or on a worksheet.

4. Groups feed back their ideas and discuss with the whole group.

Generic Starter 37:

Take a Guess

Number of people: Any.

Materials: Worksheet as explained below.

Time: 4-5 minutes.

Overview: This is a simple way to create some interest in a new topic.

Directions:

1. Before the lesson, prepare a worksheet with a list of statements – some subject-related, some off-topic. At the top of the sheet the instructions read: "Put a tick next to the sentences that are true/related to this topic."

2. Place one worksheet on each chair so that students have to read the sheet before they sit down – or issue them at the door as they enter the room.

3. Students are given a time limit to complete the sheet and then told to compare their sheet with their learning partner's.

Generic Starter 38:

Box BINGO

Overview: A great way to keep students focused during the lesson.

Number of people: Groups of two to four.

Materials: One empty cardboard box per group, paper, tape and pens.

Time: Around 5 minutes to start – carrying on through the lesson.

Directions:

1. Teacher writes the lesson title on the board and presents students with a list of twenty to thirty simple questions about the topic which are likely to be answered during the lesson. The questions are pre-written – either on a slide or sheet of paper, and given to each group to look at.

2. Each student in each group must pick ONE question (to which they don't know the answer) from the list and write it on his/her sheet of paper. They then stick their question to one of the box sides. As there are six sides to a box, some students get to write more than one question.

3. The teacher should try to keep the question sheet in front of them during the lesson to monitor which questions are asked as the lesson progresses, but the idea is that as soon as a question is answered, any student who has written this down on their team's box should write the answer on the box, under their question. When a team's questions have all been answered they can stand and shout "Box!" (or any other suitably-entertaining word).

4. A joke trophy could be awarded to the winning team (eg, a gold, spray-painted box mounted on a plinth) to create a ceremony and this could be used as a regular way of keeping students focused on the lesson topic.

Generic Starter 39:

Question Bags

Overview: Continuing with our packaging theme, here's a nice little activity to stimulate group discussion in an active format.

Number of people: Groups of up to 5 students.

Materials: Paper bags, pens and 'answer slips' (strips of card or paper).

Time: Around 5-10 minutes.

Directions:

1. Write a question on the outside of a paper bag and have enough bags for groups of four to five students – a different question on each bag. The bags should be sealed – with tape or staples – leaving a small slit wide enough to 'post' an answer slip into the bag.

2. One bag is issued to each group and students discuss their answer to the question. A designated member of the group writes the group's answer on a piece of card or paper with the group's name at the top so as to identify their answer later.

3. Bags are rotated between groups through three or four 'rounds'; ie, bags are passed from table to table so that each group gets a new bag with a new question to answer. They repeat the process of 'posting' their answer into the bag so that there are three to five different answers in each bag.

4. In the final round, each group rips open the bag they are given and they decide, as a group on the best answer before reading it out to the rest of the class. (If you have time to spare, you can leave a few days between steps 3 and 4 to simulate Royal Mail first-class post.)

Generic Starter 40:

Family Fortunes

Overview: This is a variation on a very popular TV quiz show, great fun at all ages and sure to motivate even the most challenging class. How about that for a gauntlet? Can be played as a starter/plenary or an extended mid-lesson game.

Number of people: Whole class – can be played in groups of three to six (see variation below).

Materials: A list of suitable questions (see list below).

Time: 15 minutes.

Directions:

1. Teacher reads out a question from the list.

2. Students write down the answer they think other students are most likely to give and score 1 point for every player who writes the same answer. Eg: **Q: Name a bone in the human body?**

3. Teacher then says "Put your hand up if you wrote 'Tibia'". The answers are counted and if there were ten students who wrote 'tibia' each of them would score nine.

4. The teacher then works through other major bones in the human skeleton – allocating points accordingly.

Variation:

Turn it into a team game by pitching two teams against each other and having a list of '100 most common answers' prepared for each question. Eg: For the question "Name a type of fruit" the five 'most common' answers from a survey of 100 people might be –

Team members on each team have to try and guess the most common answer and their team gets one point for each answer from the list they manage to guess.

Generic Starter 41:

Chance

Overview:

A great way to get students involved in a lesson is to give them total control. The next best thing is to give up control to a game of chance – especially if some of the chances involve some enticing things like watching a video instead of working.

This quick activity works by giving students, as rewards, the learning tasks you have already planned for the lesson. It's also a great way to get everyone into a positive mood.

Number of people: Whole class.

Materials: Any of the editable dice templates in your Resources section here:

http://needsfocusedteaching.com/kindle/starters

This particular resource would be best blown up to A3 and printed on card.

Time: A few minutes at the start of a lesson, and occasionally throughout.

Directions:

1. Decide before the lesson on six attractive activities such as 'play a game', 'watch a DVD', 'practical activity', 'group activity', 'sit and talk' etc. Plan suitable learning activities for each of these titles.

2. Any of these can be made into a useful and sensible teaching activity with some creativity: 'watch a DVD', for example, could be a 30 minute clip with an accompanying question sheet about the film which students must answer as they watch; 'sit and talk' could be a debate or discussion. Write one activity on each face of a large die.

3. Start the lesson by telling them a brief synopsis of the book 'Dice Man', about a man who decided to live his life on the roll of a dice, and that you've decided to run the lesson in the same way. It's bound to get their attention when you show them the possible activities they can 'win'. If it doesn't, add a negative category to one of the faces such as 'work in silence' or 'book work'. That should spice things up a bit!

Generic Starter 42:

Use The ONE WORD That Guarantees INSTANT Student Engagement

Overview:

Would you like to know about a teaching strategy you can use at the start of ANY lesson to gain instant engagement and participation from all your students?

I can sum this strategy up in just ONE WORD. And when you apply this word at the start of your lesson you are virtually guaranteed to hook your students straight away, get them interested and increase buy-in for the rest of your lesson content.

You can use this at the start of ANY lesson and you can use it as often as you wish.

When you use this word, you can often have students BEGGING to hear what you've got to say next.

I believe this is the best, most reliable method for starting your lessons because when you get it right, ALL your students will respond to it.

So, do you want to know what this magic word is? Maybe you've guessed already.

If you haven't guessed, I'm sure you're desperate to discover it. That's because I've used the very same technique here as an example of how effective it is.

The word is... CURIOSITY.

It's true isn't it? When your students are curious you don't have to force them to be engaged, you don't have to bribe them or demand that they take part.

By making them curious you effectively and naturally INVITE their attention.

Number of people: Whole class.

Materials: I've put together a complete training program (free for you as a gift for buying this book) on using CURIOSITY in lessons. It includes 25 different and adaptable ways of adding intrigue to your lessons and getting your students ready and eager to learn.

You can find it in your Resources section here:

http://needsfocusedteaching.com/kindle/starters

Time: A few minutes at the start of a lesson, and occasionally throughout.

Part 2

Variations on a theme: Instant Connections

Throughout the course of my work as both teacher mentor and private coach I have observed countless lessons and noticed that the majority tend to start in a very similar way, with two distinct phases. During **Phase 1** students wander in and spend time getting settled, chatting, getting equipment out, taking coats off and putting bags away. In some lessons this phase takes longer than others.

Phase 2 begins with some sort of introduction from the teacher and/or register call. Again, the time spent on this second phase varies but there is an interesting correlation: the more time spent on these two introductory phases, the more restless, bored and unsettled the students become, with less likelihood that they'll be engaged in the ensuing lesson activities.

Prevention, if you'll excuse the cliché, is better than cure - so the best thing to do to maximise the lesson's chance of success is to engage them from the moment they walk in the room.

The following 'instant connection' activities will grab attention and steer students on to connect with the lesson topic...

Instant Connection 1:

Spotty Votes

Overview:

Instantly gets students involved in the lesson topic in an active manner and has a useful plenary built in. Provides valuable assessment feedback as to the amount of learning which has taken place.

Number of people: Whole class.

Materials: Large pieces of paper – flip chart size or A3, coloured markers, packs of sticky coloured spots.

Time: 5 minutes.

Directions:

1. Prepare several charts to stick on the wall round the room. Each chart should have, written at the top, one key point or learning outcome relating to the lesson. Write out an instruction sheet which explains the following:

"When asked to do so, take two **red** dots from your activity pack and read the outcomes on the wall charts. Stick a dot underneath **two** of the outcomes which are most important to you."

2. Students can work in groups, pairs or individually. Place a strip of **red** spotty stickers and an instruction sheet on each table.

3. Give students a few minutes to place their votes and then instruct them to return to their seats to discuss with their group which outcomes they voted on, and why.

4. Link back to the charts at the end of the lesson by getting students to place a **green** spotty sticker under any outcome which they feel they have learned or has been sufficiently covered.

Instant Connection 2:

Take a Guess

Overview:

Instantly gets students involved in the lesson topic in an active and cooperative manner.

Number of people: Whole class.

Materials: Pre-written worksheet with a list of true/false-type statements. These should be mainly topic-related with a few off-topic, humorous statements thrown in for good measure. (Write the off-topic statements near the top of the list so that it doesn't just look like a long boring list to any disinterested students).

Time: 5 minutes.

Directions:

1. Place a worksheet on each student's chair or hand them out as they enter the room. The worksheet should have an introduction to the activity:

"Read the following statements. Highlight/circle/underline."

2. Start a large timer (there is a free one in your resource area) and give students three minutes to read the statements and indicate those they agree with.

3. Discuss findings as a group for five minutes.

Variation:

1. Give them a list of sentences which form part of a sequence and ask them to number them in the correct order.

2. Give them a list of sentences with missing words and ask them to fill in the blanks.

Instant Connection 3:

Walk About Survey

Overview:

Instantly gets students involved in the lesson topic in an active and cooperative manner. This is a great activity for implanting key lesson questions in the students' minds through repetition, and for discovering prior knowledge/areas of weakness.

Number of people: Whole class.

Materials: Index cards for each student. List of questions relating to the lesson content posted on charts/posters around the room or on a Power Point slide.

Time: 10 minutes.

Directions:

1. Each student is given an index card on entry to the room and told to write the seven questions from the wall charts/Power Point slide on their card (leaving room under each one for the answer). Students of lower ability may need pre-written lists of questions.

2. Students move round the room trying to find someone who knows the answer to any one of the questions. When a student answers a question they write the answer and their initials/name under the question on the card.

3. Students return to their seats and the teacher reads through the list of questions. Students raise their hands if they managed to find an answer to the question and the totals are noted. Questions with few answers are those which need to be answered during the lesson.

Part 3

Making your lessons 'unforgettable' - the power of emotions in teaching

One of the surest ways to make your lesson material 'stick' is to build review and plenary activity time into lessons. Yet, despite the obvious fact that reviewed material is much more likely to be retained than material that has not, few teachers actually plan sufficient time in their lessons to run an adequate plenary.

A rushed "What did we learn today?" as students are packing away or standing to leave does not constitute an effective review session. What will they learn from this? What will anyone gain? Can you really gauge the effect your teaching has had on your students from one quick question as the bell rings? Can you really determine who has met your objectives and who has not? If you can't, what criteria will you use for adjusting tomorrow's lesson content?

At least ten minutes needs to be included in your lesson plan for a good, interesting Plenary and the more engaging, active and fun the activity, the better. If we can link positive emotions with the material being reviewed there is more chance it will be remembered.

Remember also that the last few minutes of a lesson are the perfect time to add positive memories to your students' **Emotion Backpacks**. We use this analogy in the Needs Focused Approach™ to explain a simple truth...

...It's much easier teaching students when they arrive at your classroom in a <u>positive</u> frame of mind.

If they arrive with the feeling that the lesson (based on their previous experience) is something they will have to ENDURE for the next hour - something that is boring, irrelevant or perhaps embarrassing or difficult - their backpack will be filled with NEGATIVE emotions before they even set foot through the door.

Teaching students who have already made up their mind that they hate your lesson before it has even started is a very HARD way to teach. It's very difficult getting them to engage when they are in that state. The easy way is to have them actually LOOKING FORWARD to a lesson carrying a rucksack with a little bit of INTRIGUE, perhaps recollections of a few LAUGHS they had last lesson or a feeling of SUCCESS and ACHIEVEMENT having UNDERSTOOD a difficult concept for the first time. The **plenary** is the perfect time to cement those feelings.

Plenaries

Plenary 1:

'Review Scrabble®'

Overview: Group members create a giant Scrabble® Board, identifying what they have learned through the lesson.

Number of people: Groups of 2-6.

Materials:

Large piece of paper and a pack of different-coloured marker pens for each group

Time: Approx. 10 minutes (Can be extended into a longer activity. The first time this is played it may take longer than ten minutes. Once participants know what to do they can be encouraged to work through quite fast.)

Directions:

1. Write the lesson title/focus on the board in bold letters.

2. Explain that words can be created using the title as the base word.

3. Review the ways in which words can be written – horizontally, vertically - and that they can begin with, end with or incorporate any available letters from the title word.

4. Set a time limit – suggest 5 minutes – and ask groups to create as many words as they can using their base/title word and arranging them in any way they please on their paper. The words must be associated with the content they have just learned during the lesson.

5. After four minutes give a 'one-minute warning' and at the end of the allotted time get groups to present back briefly on their work.

Variation:

Simplify the activity by writing the title/base word vertically and asking group members to write a word which begins with each letter of the base word.

Plenary 2:

'Index Card Match & Quiz'

Overview: A very active and fun Plenary with two parts. Students first find their partner (a person holding their 'missing information') and then quiz the other class members.

Number of people: Up to 30. Possible with larger groups but extra time needs to be allocated.

Time: Approx. 15 minutes

Directions:

1. Prepare some index cards (at least enough for half the total number of participants in the group) with questions relating to the lesson content:

e.g. A for a lesson on 'digestion', one of the question cards might be...

   • Name three sources of carbohydrates

2. On separate cards write the answers for each of the question cards. In this case the answer card might read:

   • Pasta, rice, bread

3. Combine the two sets of cards and shuffle them and give one card to each student.

4. Explain that they now have to find their matching partner. If they have a question card, they must find the person who has the

answers. If they have an answer card they must find the person who has a relevant question. Once they have found their partner they must sit together.

5. When everyone is seated, members from each pair quiz the rest of the group by reading out their question card. Students put their hands up to answer and are invited to give as much information as possible before information from the answer card is fed back to the rest of the group.

Plenary 3:

'Pub Quiz'

Overview: Active and fun Plenary with competitive element. The 'rounds' of this quiz (with scoring for each round) help keep students attentive throughout the whole quiz. Having students in mixed ability teams helps include weaker students who may feel excluded. Team names bring an extra element of competitiveness and fun.

Number of people: Up to 30. Possible with larger groups but extra time needs to be allocated.

Time: Approx. 10-15 minutes depending on the number of 'rounds'.

1. **Directions**:

2. Split class into teams (preferably 4-6 students per team) and give them 1 minute to come up with a team name and to nominate their team captain.

3. Explain that there will be 3 rounds and that each round will be scored separately. Write up the team names on the board and put four columns for scores.

4. Ask 6-10 questions (depending on time) for round 1 and then get teams to swap papers with another team to mark papers as the answers are given (captains make sure there is no cheating).

5. Ask for a volunteer to act as score-keeper and get him/her to write up the score for each team.

6. Get teams to return papers to relevant teams and repeat process for round 2. From this point onwards team members usually become highly involved and competitiveness is increased as the progressive score totals show each team's positioning in the game.

Plenary 4:

Wish You Were Here

Overview: This is a novel way of encouraging peer support, building relationships and ensuring your students remember important key facts.

Number of people: Any class size.

Time: Approx. 10 minutes

Directions:

1. Divide students into pairs and issue each student with a double 'postcard template'. See your resources here:

http://needsfocusedteaching.com/kindle/starters

2. Students fill in **postcard A** by writing 3-5 key points from the lesson and drawing a quick sketch to remind them of the lesson. On **postcard B** they write the same 3-5 key points and fill in their email address.

3. Students separate the two postcards. They stick **postcard A** in their books/files as a summary and give **postcard B** to their learning partners.

4. After two weeks, learning partners send an email to each other asking them what their 3-5 key points were.

Plenary 5:

'Yes Sir/No Sir' (or 'Yes Miss/No Miss')

Overview: A really fantastic Plenary but be prepared for a lot of noise, energy and emotion. It can become quite frenzied as students help each other to review and understand the lesson material.

Number of people: Any class size

Time: Approx. 10 minutes

Directions:

1. Put two columns on the board – one titled 'Yes Sir' and the other, 'No Sir' ('Yes Miss, No Miss') with a line down the middle.

2. Ask students to tell you anything they did NOT understand during the lesson; write their comments on the board in the 'No' column.

3. Next, ask them to tell you what they DID understand and write these comments in the 'Yes' column. You now have two lists and the goal is, as a group, to try and shorten the 'No Sir/No Miss' list.

4. Deal one at a time with the points raised in the 'No' column to clarify the problem, then ask for a volunteer who did understand to explain it for the benefit of those who didn't. Everyone benefits from this. The volunteer builds his skills by becoming 'teacher', those who didn't understand receive further instruction, and those who did understand get the material reviewed or perhaps even assist in the teaching process.

5. As each 'No' is explained and understood, cross it off the list and record it in the 'Yes' column. It's empowering for students to see their understanding grow in this way.

6. Inevitably there will still be some 'No' comments left up on the board after ten minutes or so. Rather than drag the activity out too long, use these remaining points as perfect starting points for the next lesson. Leave students with questions in their minds to mull over before you next meet:

"What can I do to explain this more clearly?"

"What do you think we should do next lesson so that we all understand this?"

"How else could you find out this information without asking a teacher?

"Which bits do I need to explain again?"

Plenary 6:

'LESSON FOR SALE'

Overview: A quiet, settling Plenary which appeals to small groups and gets students to reflect deeply about what they've learned.

Number of people: Any class size

Time: Approx. 10-15 minutes

Directions:

Ask students to design an advert for today's lesson

Demonstration may be needed to explain and show the key features of an effective advert. Less able students could be given a template to fill in such as the one below.

Explain that their adverts may be used to 'sell' the lesson to other students and should include at least three things they have learned.

Plenary 7:

'Basketball'

Overview: An active, fun review which appeals particularly to challenging groups.

Number of people: Any class size

Materials: Waste paper bin, sponge ball or wad of paper, list of prepared questions

Time: Approx. 10 minutes

Directions:

1. Have teams line up perpendicular to the front of the room.

2. Explain that the first person in line is the only person who can answer the question.

3. Ask question 1.

4. The first person who answers correctly, gets a chance to shoot a basket.

5. If the shooter makes the basket, the team earns two points. If the shot misses, one point is earned.

6. Each team should rotate its players. The first person goes to the back and everybody else moves up.

7. Ask question 2 and follow the same pattern.

8. Continue through all the questions or until all members of the team have had a chance at the front.

Plenary 8:

Student as Teacher

Overview: Students take turns to come to the front of the class and re-teach a key point from the lesson.

Number of people: Any class size. Not everyone will be able to have a turn in a single lesson, so the activity can be revisited. The teacher should therefore keep a record of those who have already participated.

Materials: Props help with this activity – a teacher's gown, mortar board and cane help students 'get in' role. If the teacher has easily identifiable characteristics such as a beard, two heads, or always wears the same tie/jacket etc, props can be used to create a 'clone' of the teacher, which students find very funny.

Time: Approx. 10 minutes

Directions:

1. Explain the activity and give students a few minutes to 'plan their lesson'. (Giving students a simplified lesson plan template gives some authenticity to the activity and provides them with a handy review sheet to put in their files).

2. As well as writing the key points on their lesson plan, each student should also write down three questions which they are going to ask the rest of the class as part of their lesson. (Who, what, where, why, when & how give them a useful starting point for generating their questions). Allocate specific key points to different groups of students to prevent too much repetition when students step up to teach.

3. Ask for two or three volunteers to teach their key points and ask their questions. Other students answer the questions, as in a normal lesson, and will be given opportunity to teach in future lessons.

Plenary 9:

Gimme Five!

Overview: Students are asked to think of five responses to a range of questions asked by the teacher who walks around the room giving a 'high five' to students who succeed.

Number of people: Any class size.

Time: Approx. 15 minutes

Directions:

1. Students work individually or in pairs for five minutes (be strict on timing) to list answers to the following questions:

Five things you have done well in the lesson.

Five things you have seen other members of the class do well.

Five things you know now, but didn't know at the start of the lesson.

Five things you would like to find out more about.

Five things you could improve next lesson.

2. Students are asked to give feedback to the class and are given a 'high five' for doing so by the teacher. (Each student gives only one set of five answers from the list, to enable all students to have an opportunity to give feedback.)

3. Students put their list in their files to refer back to in future. Learning partners give each other a 'high five' to conclude the activity.

Plenary 10:

Weird Word Link-Up

Overview: A list of random words is written on the board and students have to link one of these words to the material they have learned in the lesson. This type of creative-thinking activity really appeals to some students.

Number of people: Any class size.

Time: 10-15 minutes

Directions:

1. Teacher writes a series of six random words on the board (or uses the editable dice template).

2. Students must find a connection between the random word and the lesson topic.

TRAIN - HOSPITAL - SUN - BURGER - DOG - PARTY

Plenary 11:

Spider

Overview: Students are given a spider template as a prompt to write key points from the lesson

Number of people: Any class size.

Time: 10 minutes

Directions:

1. Divide students into groups of four.

2. Draw a simple spider on the board (if you have artistic flair; two intersecting circles and eight lines sticking into them, if you don't).

3. Ask the students to write, around the spider, information about what they've learned in the lesson (one piece of information per leg).

4. If the group has more than eight pieces of information, they should disregard evolution, add more legs and try to make a centipede!

5. When groups are finished, or when the time is up, each group assigns a leader to add a piece of information to the group spider on the board.

Plenary 12:

Doubles Tennis

Overview: Doubles tennis, played in groups of four, ensures all students are involved in a fun recap of the material covered.

Number of people: Any class size.

Time: Approx. 10 minutes

Directions:

1. Divide students into groups of four.

2. Students should then form two sub-groups of two and sit across from each other.

3. The topic is written on the board: eg, 'Pride and Prejudice - Elizabeth Bennett'.

4. Each student has a turn at 'hitting the ball' by stating a simple fact about the topic; eg, Student 1 of Team 1 might say: "strong character".

5. Student 1 of Team 2 'returns the ball' by saying something else relating to the main topic: "has many sisters".

6. The topic gets lobbed back and forth until someone can no longer continue.

Plenary 13:

The Three Stooges

Overview: A brisk, cooperative review exercise.

Number of people: Any class size (but ideally divisible by 3).

Time: Approx. 10 minutes.

Directions:

1. Divide the group into sub-groups of three, and number individuals in each group one to three.

2. Write three key points or statements from the lesson on the board, and number them one to three.

3. Each 'number one' explains 'statement one' to the rest of the sub-group. The other two students in each sub-group then do the same for their corresponding statements.

Variation:

Include an extra stage before stage '3' where students of each group agree suitable answers to their assigned statement; ie, all 'number one' students develop their answer to 'statement one' whilst students in the other two groups do the same. Students then return to their original group to share their answers.

Plenary 14

Firing Squad

Overview: Students generate questions which are then used in a 'quick-fire' round.

Number of people: Any class size.

Materials: 10-20 index cards/small pieces of paper and pens for each group.

Time: Approx. 10-15 minutes.

Directions:

1. Divide students into groups of four.

2. Have each group assign a leader/spokesperson to face the firing squad.

3. Groups write down questions on their index cards, one question per card. Put all cards in a hat (remove rabbit first, if necessary) or other suitable container.

4. Group leaders take turns to come to the front and represent their teams in the 'quick-fire' round in which the teacher asks questions drawn from the hat, for one minute each.

Variation:

Have all students involved by running the 'quick-fire' round as a group quiz rather than using individual students.

Pin the Tail on the Donkey

Overview: A kinaesthetic review exercise in which students work in pairs before being given opportunity to transfer their work to the main board. Quite safe for vegetarians/donkey lovers.

Number of people: Any class size.

Time: Approx. 10-15 minutes.

Directions:

1. Issue students with suitable diagrams (or graphs, mind maps, picture sequences etc.) with labels on separate pieces of paper. Have a large version of the images displayed on the board, visible to the whole class, and a set of large labels on card.

2. Working in pairs, students are given five minutes to arrange the labels on their own diagrams (or to arrange the picture sequence in the correct order).

3. Volunteers are asked to come up to the board and put one of the large card labels on the diagram in the appropriate place.

4. Having completed the large class version of the diagram, students are given the opportunity to stick their labels in place.

Ask the Expert

Overview: Students (or the teacher) get 'in role' and take on expert status, answering questions in the 'Hot Seat'. This has the potential for development into a complete lesson activity.

Number of people: Any class size.

Time: Approx. 15 minutes.

Directions:

1. Identify two or three suitable 'roles' relating to the subject. This could be an expert on the subject or an individual linked to it in some way. A suitable expert for a science lesson on digestion, for example, could be TV nutritionist Dr Gillian McKeith. Maybe.

2. Invite students to interview for the various roles (this part would actually be done prior to the lesson).

3. Students are told that one or more experts will be available to answer their questions. All students are given five minutes to write suitable questions to put to the expert.

4. The experts are given suitable props and invited to take the 'Hot Seat' at the front of the room. Students are invited to quiz the expert with their questions.

Plenary 17:

My Brain Is Full!

Overview: Follow-up to the 'What's in my Brain?' starter activity. Students revisit their brain drawing and fill in the main points they have learned. This provides a nice visual link to the information that has been learned.

Number of people: Any class size.

Time: Approx. 5-10 minutes.

Materials: 'My Brain' templates See in your online resources, here:

http://needsfocusedteaching.com/kindle/starters

Directions:

1. Ask students to turn back to their brain templates and fill in as many spaces as they can with the main points they have learned in the lesson.

2. A large version of the template could be shown on the board, and filled in by taking feedback from the group when they have completed their own templates.

Plenary 18:

Zip It Down

Overview: Students are asked to reduce ('zip down') the content of the lesson to make it easier to remember.

Number of people: Any class size.

Time: Approx. 15-20 minutes.

Directions:

1. Divide main group up into learning partners or sub-groups of four or five.

2. Give each team ten minutes to reduce the essence of the lesson or content using one of the following techniques (examples of these techniques are to be written on the board or provided in a handout):

   - Acronym

   - Rhyme or rap verse

   - Alliteration

   - Short phrase

   - Mnemonic

3. Students present their 'zipped down' lesson content to the rest of the group.

Plenary 19:

Snakes and Ladders

Number of people: Groups up to 35

Materials: Snakes and Ladders game template. See 'Resources' here:

http://needsfocusedteaching.com/kindle/starters

This would benefit from being enlarged to A3. Dice for each group, counter for each group member and pre-written question/answer cards. Some time is required to write suitable question cards – each question should include the correct answer underneath.

Time: 10-15 minutes.

Overview: Students play Snakes and Ladders in small groups, answering questions about the lesson topic.

Directions:

1. Split class into groups of 4-5.

2. Each group is given a copy of the Snakes and Ladders board template together with dice, counters and a set of question cards.

3. Whenever a student lands on either a snake head or the foot of a ladder another group member takes a question card and reads the question. If they get the answer right on a ladder they can move up. If they get it wrong on a snake, they must move down.

Plenary 20:

Puzzle Pieces

Overview: A lesson handout becomes a novel active review puzzle when turned over. Students work in teams or pairs to solve the review puzzle.

Number of people: Any class size.

 Materials: 'Puzzle Pieces' template. See 'Resources' here:

http://needsfocusedteaching.com/kindle/starters

Time: Approx. 15 minutes.

Directions:

1. Divide main group up into pairs or sub-groups of four or five.

2. Give each student a copy of the '**Puzzle Pieces**' template, either separately or photocopied on the back of a lesson handout/ worksheet.

3. Students are asked to name the key points covered in the lesson, which are then written on the board. A total of five key points is required – the teacher may have to do some juggling to achieve this.

4. Students write one of the key points in each of the five pieces on their '**Puzzle Pieces**' template.

5. Students cut out each of the five pieces of their puzzle and attempt to assemble the pieces into the letter 'F'.

Note:

Have the letter 'F' represent a summarising word for the lesson. For a science lesson on 'Forces' this is obvious – other lesson topics will almost certainly require some creative thinking. A generic solution could be the word 'Fail', which students are told will be the result of not completing the activity.

Plenary 21:

Blockbusters

Overview: A great interactive review game based on the popular TV programme of the same name. The object of the game is for your team to work their way across the board from one side to the other by answering questions correctly. Can be used for whole-topic revision or keyword reviews.

Number of people: Any class size; class is split into two groups – around thirty to thirty five would be the maximum total.

Materials: Blockbusters PowerPoint presentation/Interactive Whiteboard game template See 'Whiteboard Resources', online here:

http://needsfocusedteaching.com/kindle/starters

Some time is required to pre-set the template with initial letters and clues, and to don the Bob Holness wig and glasses (optional).

Time: Approx. 10-15 minutes.

Directions:

Prepare a list of at least twenty questions relating to the lesson topic. The answers to the questions should be 'one word' answers, eg:

Q. What is the common name for sodium chloride?

A. Salt

Fill in the template by allocating the initial of each answer to a separate hexagon.

Split the class into two groups – the yellow team have a slight advantage in that they don't have as far to travel so allocate this colour to the team with fewer members, or the team who has worked best throughout the lesson.

The yellow team get to go first and a spokesperson for the team picks a letter to start, eg:

> *"Can I have a 'P' please sir?"*

Once the inevitable guffaws have subsided, the teacher then reads out the question:

> *"What 'P' is a fake medical intervention?"*

Members of the team raise their hands to answer and if they get it right the hexagon turns to colour of their team – blue or yellow. This is achieved by the teacher 'left clicking' the hexagon when the presentation is in slideshow mode – click once to turn it blue and twice to turn it yellow.

If the team gets the answer correct they get to pick another letter to continue their journey across the board. Each team is only permitted to pick a letter in an adjacent hexagon to one they already 'own'.

If the team answers incorrectly play is passed to the other team.

A team wins the game when they have managed to join one side of the board with the other in their respective colour.

Plenary 22

Cooperative Cards™ - REVIEWS

Number of people: Teams of three to six

Materials: A set of cooperative review cards. See 'Whiteboard Resources' in your online Resources here:

Time: 5-10 minutes.

Overview: Students work in their learning teams to review the lesson content by taking turns to answer questions on the review cards.

Directions:

1. Split class into groups of 3-6.

2. Give each group a set of Cooperative Review Cards.

3. Use cards in one of the following ways...

A) Take-A-Turn

Cards are placed in a stack, face down in the centre of the group's table. Students in each team take turns to pick a card and respond to the question.

B) Pick-A-Card

The cards are spread out, face upwards, in the centre of the table. The first student chooses a card and responds to the question. Play then passes to the other students. Once a card has been chosen it must be turned face down.

C) All Respond - Team

Cards are placed face down on the team's table. One student picks a card and reads out the question. Each student in the team must then respond by writing their own answer to the question. Students then share/compare their answers before the next student picks another card.

D) All respond – Whole class

As a whole class activity a student is chosen to pick a random review card. The teacher reads the question and each student responds by writing their answer on a small white board or piece of paper. Answers are shared and compared.

E) Delegate

Cards are placed in the centre of the team's table. Each student is given a 'DELEGATE' card and may use it to pass play to another team mate of they are unable to answer the question.

Plenary 23:

Time Line

Number of people: Unlimited

Materials: String, Blu-tak, A4 paper, post-it notes, scissors

Time: 10-20 minutes

Overview:

Students work in groups and use a physical timeline to share a visual representation of significant points in a unit of study. This activity can also be used on an individual basis as a 'getting to know you activity' where students use the timeline to represent major events in their personal lives from birth to present day.

Instructions:

1. Ask students to write the start date of the unit of study on one piece of A4 paper and 'Present time' on another.

2. Tell each group to stick their two pieces of paper up as a time line (with string in between) somewhere in the room where they can be clearly seen, approximately three metres apart (depending on the number of students/size of room).

3. Hand out a pad of post-it notes to each group. Tell them to discuss the major findings/key points from the lesson and to add them to their timeline in the order in which they happened.

4. Ask groups to share their timelines with the rest of the class

Variation:

If running this activity as a 'getting to know you' activity with personal timelines of students' lives, at step 4 above students should wander around 'gallery style' and ask about each other's timelines and then be encouraged to share them with the group as a whole.

Plenary 24:

The Maze

Number of people: Unlimited

Materials: Maze Sheet (See 'Resources')

Time: 10 minutes

Overview:

Students work independently, solving a maze puzzle to reach the lesson objective before adding key points they've learned along the way.

Instructions:

1. Issue students with a copy of 'The Maze'.

2. Students write the learning objective in the centre space and then work out the correct route to the objective from outside the maze.

3. Once students have identified the correct route they write along their route the key points or facts they have learned during the lesson to reach the lesson objective.

Building Blocks

Number of people: Class of around 30-35 is optimum.

Materials: None required.

Time: 10 - 15 minutes.

Overview: Students work together in teams to collect information relating to the topic.

Directions:

1. Students are arranged in teams of four.

2. Team members are numbered 1-4 and each is given a question according to their number, relating to the lesson content – ie, all 1s are given question one, all 2s are given question two and so on.

3. Students are given two minutes to answer their individual question as best they can.

4. After two minutes a hooter signifies the end of the first round and students pass their papers to the team mate on their right.

5. Each member then adds something to the answer that has been handed to them; allow up to one minute for this part. This process continues until all team mates have added content to each of the four questions.

6. Teacher reads out each question in turn and each team is given the opportunity to answer from the combined answers on their sheets. Each new piece of information is added on the board under the relevant question.

7. Students use the information on the board (the combined answer of the whole class) to write a model answer for the question.

Variation:

Teams work through points 6 and 7 on their own.

Plenary 26:

Eliminator

Number of people: Works best with small classes of 5-20.

Materials: None required.

Time: 5-10 minutes.

Overview: Students try to beat the teacher by naming key points from the lesson.

Directions:

1. Teacher writes down 10 keywords from the lesson on a sheet of paper. To make the game more visual the words can be written on pieces of card and stuck on the board, face down.

2. Students have to call out keywords/facts relating to the lesson topic.

3. The teacher crosses off words as they are called out (or, if the 'card on the board' method is used, the teacher turns the relevant card over) – the aim being to get the teacher to cross off all the key words within three minutes.

4. Repeat by reversing roles – you try to guess key words from a list compiled by the students.

Ready, Steady, 'Teach'

Number of people: Any.

Materials: A wide selection of odd props. Model-making materials such as cardboard boxes, string, cardboard tubes, wire coat hangers, lollypop sticks etc are a good start but everyday items such as clothing, hats, cooking utensils, kitchen sink and general tools could also be included. A selection of items is placed in a plastic 'shopping' bag.

Time: 15 minutes.

Overview: Teams of students have five minutes to plan an activity in which they use the shopping bag contents to 'teach' the rest of the class the main points of the lesson. This activity is the perfect plenary choice for students who enjoy role-play and a chance to show off. Split the activity over two or three lessons so as to give each team a chance to do the teaching without encroaching on too much lesson time. Consider filming each team (after obtaining permission from parents) – the finished films will provide a humorous revision activity later in the year.

Directions:

1. Students form teams of three or four.

2. Teacher writes a selection of four or five key points from the lesson/ scheme of work on the board.

3. Each team is given a box or shopping bag of props and five minutes to plan an activity in which they use the shopping bag contents to teach the rest of the class any one of the key points from the board.

4. Teams take it in turns to teach the class.

Plenary 28:

Sell it!

Number of people: Any.

Materials: None required.

Time: 15 minutes.

Overview: Basically, this activity just involves students relaying the key points or features from a unit of study/lesson. However, with a little twist and some theatrical fairy- dust it is magically transformed into something far more fun than repeating facts 'parrot fashion'.

Directions:

1. Students form teams of three or four.

2. Teacher writes a selection of features/key points relating to the lesson/subject topic.

3. Teams are given five minutes to prepare a sales message for one of the features from the board.

It may be necessary to give teams a writing frame or at least sentence prompts such as:

"We think _____ is a fantastic idea because...."

"_____ is well suited to any market because..."

"You should buy _____ because..."

"The main features of _____ are..."

"The best thing about_____ is..."

"_____ can help with (insert appropriate cause or relevant problem) due to..."

Plenary 29:

Plan it!

Number of people: Any.

Materials: None required.

Time: 15 minutes.

Overview: The most creative people in your classroom are undoubtedly the students themselves. This activity makes use of their talents while giving students some ownership of lesson activities and providing a means for them to recap important information in a fun way. In effect the students plan a starter activity for the next lesson.

Directions:

1. Students form teams of three or four.

2. Criteria and instructions are written on the board (or a 'mission sheet' and sealed in an envelope).

Further instructions might include:

- The activity must allow class members to interact with the teacher and provide answers to questions in some way.

- The activity must last between five and ten minutes.

- The activity must include the following key points...

Some groups will require more guidance than others but care should be taken not to stifle their creativity by being too rigid.

3. Teams are given fifteen minutes to plan a starter (or plenary) activity for the next lesson which will recap and revisit skills from the current lesson content.

4. Either use one or more of the starters as an actual starter for the next lesson, or allow groups to 'teach' their starters themselves.

Plenary 30:

Aliens & Defenders

Number of people: Class divided into two groups with one captain each.

Materials: Interactive PowerPoint-based game. See 'Whiteboard Resources' in your internet resources here:

http://needsfocusedteaching.com/kindle/starters

Time: 5-10 minutes (a little bit longer the first time).

Overview: Class is divided in two groups: alien invaders and earth defenders. Using the interactive PowerPoint-based game in Whiteboard Resources, students are asked questions to assess what they have learned through the lesson.

Directions:

1. Divide the class into two groups: alien invaders and earth defenders.

2. Select one captain for each team; they sit at the front. If you can give them space helmets and toy phasers, so much the better.

3. Launch the Interactive PowerPoint-based game.

4. Ask one question in turn, related to the lesson of course, to each captain. They need to nominate a different member of their team each time to answer the questions. The captains themselves will answer the final question to win or lose.

5. Each time a team gets the answer right, they destroy one of the other team's spaceships. If they get it wrong, they destroy one of their own spaceships.

6. The winner team is the team that destroys all of the other team's spaceships.

7. Instructions for the game activity are on the game slides to make things easier:

Variation:

It could be made part of a carousel lesson, with other activities included in the session. This could add an extra kinaesthetic and visual element.

Plenary 31:

Memory Game

Number of people: Any.

Materials: Sugar paper and marker pens.

Time: 10-15 minutes.

Overview: A terrific team-building plenary, adaptable to most areas of the curriculum. Students work in small groups to recall facts from the lesson.

Directions:

1. Split the class into teams of four. Each team member is given a number – one to four.

2. Teacher calls out "ones!" and all the ones come to the front desk to look at, and memorise, as much as they can from the map/ sequences/plan/diagram/chart/storyboard in a given time.

3. The 'ones' then go back to their groups and record on paper what they can remember within a given time limit.

4. Teacher calls out "twos" and the 'twos' from each group come up to the front desk to take a turn at trying to memorise more of the information. They then go back to their groups and record extra information to add to, and improve, the first attempt by the 'ones'.

5. The process is repeated for the threes and fours.

6. Each group comes to the front to present their version of the original material.

Plenary 32:

Chuck

Number of people: Small/medium groups of 6-20 participants are best although it is possible to run this with larger groups as well.

Materials: Suitable VST (Volunteer Selection Tool) – a stuffed toy, sponge ball, Koosh® Ball, bean bag etc. Boomerangs are not recommended.

Time: 10-15 minutes.

Overview: A high-energy closing activity to finish on a high after a lesson with a small to medium sized group. Relates best to social studies-type lesson topics as students will be relaying how they will use new skills information in future.

Directions:

1. Tell students you are holding a VST in your hand (a 'Volunteer Selection Tool').

2. Arrange students in a circle, standing facing each other.

3. Tell students that when they catch the item they must say two things:

- What they enjoyed about the lesson – what they appreciated about the other group members or the learning experience

- How they plan to put what they've learned into action in future

4. Students can repeat what someone else has already said – to encourage those who wouldn't normally take part to participate.

5. Once a student has made comments they then throw the item to someone else in the circle.

Plenary 33:

On air!

Number of people: Small/medium groups of 6-20 participants are best purely because of the amount of time taken to 'show back' to the rest of the group.

Materials: Suitable props can transform this into a full lesson activity although with practice, once students know what is expected of them, the activity can be completed relatively quickly.

Time: 10-15 minutes.

Overview: A high-energy closing activity to finish on a high after a lesson with a small to medium sized group. Relates best to social studies-type lesson topics as students will be relaying how they will use new skills information in future.

Directions:

1. Split the class into groups of four and number each member of the group from one to four.

2. Teacher gives each group a main topic from the lesson on which to present a very short news item.

3. Roles are as follows:

Ones: Announces the headline (ie, the particular stage of the cycle/chapter summary/character description that their group will be reporting about). A 'News at Ten' gong could be sounded between each headline.

Twos: Reads a summary of the group's 'news' (chapter/sequence stage/character review etc.) in the style of a studio newsreader before handing over to the 'roving reporter'.

Threes: Roving reporter – sits in another part of the room and gives more details on the group's 'story' and also interviews the 'witness' or 'subject expert'.

Fours: Witness/subject expert – gives further information to embellish the group's knowledge of the topic.

Plenary 34:

Plenary Triangle

Number of people: Any group size – students work individually, in pairs or in small groups

Materials: Provide students with a blank triangle template or get them to draw their own as part of the exercise

Time: 10-15 minutes

1 = What do you remember from the last lesson?

2 = What have you learnt today?

3 = What question would you ask someone to check their learning?

4 = Summarize today's lesson in three Words.

Directions:

1. Ask and allow students to think about what they remember from previous lessons, what they have learnt or been reminded about today, a question to ask the someone else about the lesson and summarise their learning today in 3 key words.

2. Students will do this using the plenary triangle with simple instructions on the board and a blank template provided to them (see below for both).

3. Students are selected to share their answers/opinions with the class or small groups.

Plenary 35:

Review Relay

Number of people: any group size up to 40 max.

Materials: Coloured pens and flipchart paper

Time: 10-15 minutes

Overview: A high-energy physical review – good for engaging unmotivated students.

Directions:

1. Divide the class into three or four teams, depending on numbers, of up to ten students.

2. Give each team a different coloured marker (red/blue/green/black) and get teams to think of a team name for comedy value.

3. Put three or four pieces of flipchart paper on the board/wall with team names written at the top in the relevant colour.

4. One person from each team starts by writing on their team paper one thing they have learned during the lesson. They come back, hand the pen to another person in their team and then the second person writes something they have learned (It must be different from the previous ones). The winning team is the one with the most new things learned.

NB:

Teacher can **differentiate** by making sure less able children are at the front of each line and more able towards the end – it obviously gets harder to think of additional facts as the game progresses.

Plenary 36:

Target

Number of people: any group size

Materials: N/A

Time: 10-15 minutes

Overview: This reflective activity encourages students to think about and provide answers to the question 'How can I improve my work?' – identifying specific and achievable steps to take next lesson. Activities like this are very important if students are to feel they are making progress. Many are not aware what they should or could be doing in order to improve. It is a very positive way to end a lesson.

Directions:

1. Give five minutes for students to think what small single step they could take next lesson in order to improve.

2. In some instances it may be useful to provide students with a written list of targets

3. Try varying the focus of the target each week and have a corresponding list of targets for each focus. E.g. Week 1 Presentation: 'Label axes on graphs', 'Use pencil for diagrams', 'Underline headings' Week 2 Behaviour: 'Stay in my own seat', 'Put my hand up to ask a question', 'Bring all necessary equipment to class', Week 3 answering questions: 'Read questions thoroughly' etc.

4. At the end of the following week ask students to consider how well they completed their target.

Variation:

Ask students to work with their learning partner and them to suggest a target for their peer.

Plenary 37:

Txt Spk

Overview: Very simple review which will appeal to your students – especially the little darlings who insist on using their mobile phones in class.

Number of people: any group size.

Materials: None – they bring it!

Time: 10 minutes.

Directions:

1. Students work independently, writing two or three main points learned during the lesson using TEXT shortcuts.

2. Pick some of the most creative attempts and have students write them up on the board or add to a continual 'What we are learning' display.

Plenary 38:

Bullseye

Overview: This is a simplified version of the classic 80's TV game show of the same name. (If you missed it, it involved a darts player throwing darts, a contestant bumbling through questions, and comedian Jim Bowen enthusing over fabulous prizes which invariably included the same speedboat every week. It was the stuff of television legend and transcended its humble Sunday evening quiz origins to become a national institution, albeit one constructed entirely of cardboard and glitter. Now your lessons can follow in its footsteps, and if you give Jim a call they probably even still have the boat.)

Number of people: any group size.

Materials: Dartboard and darts. I highly recommend the magnetic or sticky felt type, since the traditional ones can make rather a mess of students.

Time: 10-15 minutes.

Directions:

1. Set up the board as per the diagram. For every two sections of the board you have a named category. The categories should be related to the lesson or subject although it's good to also throw in a fun category too such as Music, Soaps, 16th century German philosophers etc, as well as the odd forfeit such as 'extra homework'. If anyone hits the bull you could give them 'Bully's Special Prize' (see Jim Bowen's Catch Phrases below) like an early finish. Or that speedboat.

2. Students play in pairs, alternating between dart-throwing and question-answering. Allow each pair to come to the front of the class and take their turn. Student A throws the dart and then student B must answer a question from the relevant category chosen by student A's dart. They then swap places.

3. There is obviously a limit to the number of rounds you can play. I find it works best as a regular event at the end of every lesson, for a few days or weeks. Keep a rolling total of scores on the wall in a corner of the room, throw in some prizes and consolation prizes (remember the 'Bendy Bully'?) and you'll find it becomes a very popular ongoing competition.

Here are some Jim Bowen catchphrases to add authenticity to your show, if you want to really immerse yourself in the part. Better dust off your best Yorkshire accent!

The show always starts with the cry of: "It's a bulllllseye! And here's your host - Jiiiim Bowen!"

"Keep out of the black and in the red, nothing in this game for two in a bed."

"Super, smashing, great."

"You win nothing but your BFH... Bus Fare Home"

(into the ad break) "I've got £____ here and it'll take me two minutes to count out."

"...And the category's gone, so I can't ask the question!"

"Up to the oche - and listen to Tony!"

"Let's check that with Bully" (for the spelling category)

"The subjects that are lit are the ones you can hit!"

"You've had a good night out - but you go home with nowt!"

"Throwers and knowers" (dart players and question answerers)

Yes, today's light entertainment makers would do well to study old videotapes.

Plenary 39:

In The Style of...

Overview: A very quick-to-set-up and often hilarious Plenary. Can be used at any stage of a lesson during question/answer phases to inject some humour and develop confidence in students.

Number of people: any group size.

Materials: None required although the activity can be taken a stage further by including 'Style of...' dice. There's a template in your resource area, online here:

http://needsfocusedteaching.com/kindle/starters

Time: 10 minutes.

Directions:

1. Ask a review question about the lesson topic.

2. Ask students to either respond in a nominated style (see below) or roll the 'Style of..' die.

Suggested styles:

- Newsreader

- Monk (Gregorian chant)

- Builder

- Dracula

- Very happy person (lottery/speedboat winner)

- Miserable person (lottery loser)

- Angry person (lottery winner who has had his/her ticket stolen)

- Very boring person

- Superhero

- Farmer

- Mad scientist

- Weather girl/man

- Pilot

- Rock Star

- Children's TV presenter

- Mime

Plenary 40:

Mirror Writing

Overview: A simple, quick review that gets students thinking about the topic you've covered. What more could you want?

Number of people: any group size.

Materials: N/A

Time: 10-15 minutes.

Directions:

1. Students work in pairs or small groups.

2. Each student writes three key things they've learnt during the lesson. In a shocking twist, they write the facts backwards – in mirror writing!

3. Students then swap papers with their partners or other group members and try to decipher what each has written.

Mark the Exam

Overview: Very simple but can be good fun – depending on how creative you are with the 'spoof answers'.

Number of people: any group size.

Materials: Real or made up sample exam papers on the lesson topic.

Time: 10-15 minutes.

Directions:

1. Students work in groups or pairs.

2. Each pair or team is given a sample past exam paper (this can be a real one or a 'home made' set of questions) which has been carefully completed by a fictitious student.

3. Students work together to spot the errors and correct them.

Vision On

Overview: Those of you old enough to have owned a steam-driven television may fondly remember Tony Hart's wonderful art program for youngsters in the 70's – 'Vision On' – and his regular showing of viewers artwork in 'The Gallery'. This activity is a brilliant, visual way to sum up students' learning in a lesson and, if used regularly, can also provide an ongoing record of an entire term's work for revision purposes. If you can get a download of the Vision On theme tune, all the better (at time of going to press, the mp3 is only 79p from Amazon).

Number of people: Any group size.

Materials: A3-size sheets of paper, rough scraps of paper and coloured pens/markers for each table group.

Time: 10 minutes.

Directions:

1. Students work in groups, pairs or individually.

2. Each table group is given a set of coloured marker pens and some sheets of A3 paper. (A3 paper is used for the final piece - to keep diagrams small and succinct – so that all work can be displayed easily. The scraps of paper are for rough work).

3. Students have five minutes to work out (in rough on the scraps of paper) a simple, creative picture which sums up the day's learning. The more punchy and striking the better – simple cartoons and stick figures work well - but detailed concept maps, spider diagrams and abstract images are also to be encouraged if that is the way the student prefers to remember the work. Diagrams must not contain words.

4. Allow the students another five minutes to complete their finished design using the A3 paper, then display the finished pieces on the wall under a suitable heading. Now would be a great time to play the 'Vision On' theme tune.

And... Action!

Overview: An easy-to-set-up, fast, funny and very effective review which involves everyone and capitalises on students' natural desire to show off in front of each other.

Number of people: Any group size.

Materials: None required.

Time: 10 - 15 minutes.

Directions:

1. Students work in groups of four or five.

2. Tell groups they have just three minutes to brainstorm anything and everything they have learned during the lesson. Go!

3. Get one of the groups up to the front and tell them they have just one minute to act out everything they have learned during the lesson (for some students it will be enough for them to mime the words they thought of during the brainstorming session). Audience members try to spot key words and lesson objectives as they are acted out.

4. Pick another group to come to the front and repeat.

Plenary 44:

Evidence Sheet

Overview: A ready-made prompt sheet makes this a very easy activity to set up and run. Students will enjoy the simplicity and the fact that it is linked to a real-life scenario they find intriguing yet will hopefully want to avoid – being arrested.

Number of people: Any group size.

Materials: Criminal Evidence Sheet mock-up for each student. See in your online resources, here:

http://needsfocusedteaching.com/kindle/starters

Time: 10 - 15 minutes.

Directions:

1. Students work individually or in pairs to fill in their sheets, taking time to write all the key pieces of information they have learned during the lesson in the 'evidence' section.

2. To make the activity more authentic students are encouraged to fill in the other boxes as well as giving a thumb print (fingerprint ink can be easily replicated using a felt tip or ball point pen to ink up the thumb).

3. Remind students that they are now on a criminal register - and can no longer get away with avoiding homework!

4. Snicker in evil, sinister fashion.

Plenary 45:

Partners in Crime

Overview: Continuing with our criminal theme here's a fantastic activity for getting students to work collaboratively - because they have no choice! From the point of view of ensuring learning takes place this is one of the best review activities.

Number of people: Any group size.

Materials: 10 straight forward test questions based on the lesson content.

Time: 10 - 15 minutes.

Directions:

1. Students work in pairs.

2. Tell students they have five minutes to go through the day's lesson content with their partner because there is going to be a short test, the results of which will determine how much homework they receive.

3. Place a graph on the wall/board showing scores as percentages (10%-100%) with corresponding homework assignments (from '100% = no homework' down to '10% = 10 homework questions' or similar).

4. After the five minutes' preparation time, tell students only one person from each pair will sit the test and that they will be sharing the mark their partner achieves. Get them to decide which of them will sit the test. This can be done by flipping a coin, volunteering, mud wrestling etc.

5. Once they have decided and are sitting contentedly (having volunteered the most able student to sit the test) tell them that the other partner will actually be the one to complete the task.

6. The first time you try this there won't be much collaboration (unless of course you explain what you have planned in full at the start) but in subsequent lessons you can be sure partners will work hard to make sure they have both retained as much as possible from the lesson.

Time Out

Overview: A fun variation on the popular lesson game 'Who Wants To Be A Millionaire' (itself inspired by the TV show of the same name) in which the prize is... time. It can be time out of lessons (an early finish), free time on a computer or preferred activity etc.

Number of people: Any group size.

Materials: Progressively more difficult, pre-written questions (some topic-related, some purely just for fun) each corresponding to a unit of time thus:

Question 1 (very easy)   =15 seconds free time

Question 2 (easy)   = 30 seconds free time

Question 3 (fairly easy) = 1 minute free time, and so on

Have the hardest question carry a reward of 10-15 minutes free time.

Time: 10 - 15 minutes per lesson. It is unlikely a whole game would be played in one lesson as it takes too long, but it can be spread over a series of lessons with the prize being awarded at the end of the week.

Directions:

1. Students work as one group and nominate a student to answer a question. (A student may answer one question only – once they have answered, they may not answer a later question).

2. Provide three life-lines: Phone a Friend, 50:50, Ask the Audience as per the TV show although these could be altered slightly: Phone a Parent, Ask Another Class, Ask a Teacher etc.

3. Ask two or three questions at the end of each lesson culminating with the final question at the end of the week. (I always try to

'doctor' the questions so that students get as far along the question trail as possible, to win a sufficiently motivating amount of time at the end).

Part 4

"It made my naughtiest student as quiet as a mouse!"

"Thank you so much for the superbly wonderful videos! I benefited a lot from your creative secret agent method! It made my naughtiest student as quiet as a mouse! THANK YOU..."

Yasaman Shafiee (Take Control of the Noisy Class customer)

Take Control of The Noisy Class

To get your copy, go here:

https://www.amazon.co.uk/Take-Control-Noisy-Class-Super-effective/dp/1785830082/

Also, if you'd like to receive my FREE **Behaviour Tips** on an inconsistent and irregular basis via my email service, just sign up for your free book resources and you'll start receiving my Behaviour Tips.

http://needsfocusedteaching.com/kindle/starters

These contain short, practical ideas and strategies for responding to all kinds of inappropriate classroom behaviour, as well as some handy teaching tips and ideas for improving student engagement. All this will be sent direct to your email inbox once or twice a week, along with occasional notifications about some of our other products, special offers etc.

Obviously, you can opt out of this service any time you wish but in our experience, most people pick up a lot of *wonderful* ideas from these emails. And feel free to forward the messages and resources on to other teachers (staff meetings, staff room, pop them into your Christmas cards etc.).

Just remember to look out for emails from '***Needs Focused Teaching***' so that you don't miss all the goodies.

"Thanks a million. As a fresh teacher, I find this invaluable."

"Finally something concrete and applicable in real life – I've had enough of the people who have never set their foot in a real classroom but know how everything should be done in theory. Thanks a million. As a fresh teacher, I find this invaluable."

Jasna (Take Control of the Noisy Class customer)

Final Reminder!

If you haven't already done so, head on over to the FREE resources page:

http://needsfocusedteaching.com/kindle/starters

One more thing... Please help me get this book to as many teachers as possible, by leaving an honest review...

"I have seen nothing short of miracles occur."

"I have seen nothing short of miracles occur. My students' attitudes and behaviours have improved; they are excited and personally involved in their educational experience! What more could I ask? My E books have become my bible!!! I truly am a disciple!!!!! Love you guys."

Dawn (NeedsFocusedTeaching customer)

Review Request

If you enjoyed this book, please leave me an honest review! Your support really does matter and it really does make a difference. I do read all the reviews so I can get your feedback and I do make changes as a result of that feedback.

If you'd like to leave a review, then all you need to do is go to the review section on the book's Amazon page. You'll see a big button that states "Write a customer review". Click on that and you're good to go!

You can also use the following links to locate the book on Amazon:

https://www.amazon.co.uk/dp/B073RTTLF2

https://www.amazon.com/dp/B073RTTLF2

For all other countries, please head over to the relevant Amazon site and either search for the book title or simply copy and paste the following code in the Amazon search bar to be taken directly to the book:

B073RTTLF2

Have fun and thanks for your support...

Rob

"Thank you so much Rob for what you are doing for the profession, your strategies work wonders! I have never tried the 'pen' but will do next time! Seriously speaking, I give the link to your productions to many young teachers I know because they are so unhappy sometimes and they need help which they find with what you do! So, thanks again and carry on with your good job!"

Marie (Take Control of the Noisy Class customer)

Suggested resource providers

Name: HowtoLearn.com and HowtoLearn.teachable.com

Specialty: Personalized Learning Assessments, Learning Solutions, Courses for Teachers, Parents and Students.

Website: www.HowtoLearn.com

Details: Online since 1996, the brainchild of best-selling author and college professor, Pat Wyman, known as America's Most Trusted Learning Expert. We invite you to become part of our global community and closed Facebook group. Your Learning Questions Answered at http://www.HowtoLearn.com/your-learning-questions-answered.

Resources: Take our Free Learning Styles Quiz at HowtoLearn.com and check out parent/teacher tested and approved courses at HowtoLearn.teachable.com.

* * *

Name: Time Savers for Teachers (Stevan Krajnjan)

Speciality: Resources guaranteed to save you time.

Website: http://www.timesaversforteachers.com/ashop/affiliate.php?id=7

Details: Popular forms, printable and interactive teacher resources that save time. Stevan Krajnjan was presented with an Exceptional Teacher Award by The Learning Disabilities Association of Mississauga and North Peel in recognition for outstanding work with children who have learning disabilities.

Resources: www.timesaversforteachers.com

* * *

Name: Nicola Morgan (NSM Training & Consultancy).

Speciality: Innovative resources to motivate staff and empower schools.

Website: www.nsmtc.co.uk

Details: NSM Training & Consultancy provides high quality training for teaching/non teaching staff in the UK and internationally. We provide a large range of courses, expert consultancy and guidance, publications, conferences as well as innovative resources to motivate staff and empower schools.

Resources: http://www.nsmtc.co.uk/resources/

* * *

Name: Susan Fitzell

Speciality: Special Education Needs

Website: www.SusanFitzell.com

Details: Seminar Handouts and supplemental resources for Differentiated Instruction, Motivation, Special Education Needs, Co-teaching, and more.

Resources: http://downloads.susanfitzell.com/

* * *

Name: Patricia Hensley

Speciality: Special Education

Website: http://successfulteaching.net

Details: Strategies and ideas for all grade levels. Great resource for new and struggling teachers.

Resources: Free Student Job Description. https://successfulteaching.blogspot.com/2007/10/student-job-description.html

*   *   *

Name: Julia G. Thompson

Speciality: Educational consultant, writer, and presenter.

Website: www.juliagthompson.com.

Details: Author of The First-Year Teacher's Survival Guide, Julia G Thompson specializes in assisting new teachers learn to thrive in their new profession.

Resources: For 57 free forms and templates to make your school year easier, just click go to her website and click on the Professional Binder page

*   *   *

Name: Steve Reifman

Speciality: Teaching the Whole Child (Empowering Classroom Management & Improving Student Learning)

Website: www.stevereifman.com

Details: National Board Certified Elementary Teacher & Amazon Best-Selling Author.

Author of '10 Steps to Empowering Classroom Management: Build a Productive, Cooperative Culture Without Using Rewards'

Resources: https://www.youtube.com/user/sreifman (FREE, 1-2 minute videos with tips for teachers & parents)

*   *   *

Name: Dave Vizard

Speciality: Behaviour Management

Website: www.behavioursolutions.com

Details: Creator of Brain Break materials and Ways to Manage Challenging Behaviour ebook.

Resources: www.behavioursolutions.myshopify.com/pages/brain-breaks

*   *   *

Name: Marjan Glavac

Specialty: Tips on getting a teaching job (resume, cover letter, interviews); classroom management strategies.

Website: www.thebusyeducator.com

Details: Marjan Glavac is a best selling motivational author, engaging speaker and elementary classroom teacher with over 29 years of teaching experience.

Resources: Free weekly newsletter, 4 free eBooks (http:// thebusyeducator.com/homepage.htm)

*　*　*

Name: Dr. Rich Allen

Specialty: Workshops and keynotes on engagement strategies for students of all ages

Website: greenlighteducation.net

Details: Author of 'Green Light Teaching' and 'The Rock 'n Roll Classroom'

Resources: Please join our Teaching tips community and access lots of free resources and ideas for your classroom by clicking HERE.

*　*　*

Name: Ross Morrison McGill

Speciality: Managing director at TeacherToolkit Ltd.

Website: https://www.teachertoolkit.co.uk/

Details: Ross Morrison McGill is a deputy headteacher working in an inner-city school in North London. He is the Most Followed Teacher on Twitter in the UK and writes the Most Influential Blog on Education in the UK.

Resources: https://www.amazon.co.uk/Ross-Morrison-McGill/e/B00G33GTEO/ref=dp_byline_cont_book_1

What people say about us

"Even if you have never had "the class from hell", there is something here for you"

"As a PGCE student it is great to have the opportunity to pick up user-friendly and easily accessible information. The 'Behaviour Needs' course provides exactly that. In a series of amusing, creative, fast-paced sections, Rob Plevin builds up a staggering amount of practical and thought provoking material on classroom behaviour management. All of which are easily translated back in the classroom. Even if you have never had "the class from hell", there is something here for you and the follow up information from the website is laden with golden nuggets which will give you loads more ideas and interventions."

Steve Edwards (Workshop Attendee and Take Control of the Noisy Class customer)

* * *

"I want you to know that you have changed the lives of 40 of my students."

"What an informative day. The sessions on positive reinforcement and the importance of relationships were particularly memorable. I want you to know that you have changed the lives of 40 of my students. Thank you!"

Joanne W. (Singapore Workshop Attendee)

*   *   *

"...We will be inviting Rob back on every possible occasion to work with all of our participants and trainees."

"We were delighted to be able to get Rob Plevin in to work with our Teach First participants. From the start his dynamic approach captivated the group and they were enthralled throughout. Rob covered crucial issues relating to behaviour management thoroughly and worked wonders in addressing the participants' concerns about teaching in some of the most challenging schools in the country. We will be inviting Rob back on every possible occasion to work with all of our participants and trainees."

Terry Hudson, (Regional Director 'Teach First', Sheffield Hallam University)

*   *   *

"Thank you for helping me to be in more control."

"Rob, thank you very much for sharing your experience and reminding of these simple but effective things to do. Students' behaviour (or actually my inability to control it) is so frustrating that at times it feels that nothing can help. Thank you for helping me to be in more control."

Natasha Grydasova (*Take Control of the Noisy Class* customer)

*   *   *

"I am HAPPILY spending my Sat afternoon listening, watching and reading all your extremely helpful information!"

"Thank You Rob! What a wealth of excellent ideas! This is my 30th year teaching! You would think after 30 years teaching that I wouldn't need to be viewing your awesome videos and reading your helpful blog and website. However, I am HAPPILY spending my Sat afternoon listening, watching and reading all your extremely helpful information! Thank You So Much! I will be one of your biggest fans from now on!"

Kelly Turk (Needs Focused Video Pack customer)

*   *   *

"...terrific for those teachers who are frustrated."

"Great easy-to-listen-to video tips that will be terrific for those teachers who are frustrated.

I'm forwarding this email on to the principals in my district right away!"

Sumner price (Take Control of the Noisy Class customer)

* * *

"Many thanks for all these really helpful life-savers!"

"Very many thanks. I have given myself trouble by letting kids into the room in a restless state with inevitable waste of teaching time. Your advice on calming them down in a positive, non-confrontational way and building rapport is very timely. Many thanks for all these really helpful life-savers!"

Philip Rozario (Take Control of the Noisy Class customer)

* * *

"Fantastic way to create a calm and secure learning environment for all the students."

"Thanks so much Rob. Fantastic way to create a calm and secure learning environment for all the students. It's great how you model the way we should interact with the students – firmly but always with respect."

Marion (Take Control of the Noisy Class customer)

*   *   *

"I will be recommending that the teachers in training that I deal with should have a look at these videos."

These tips and hints are put in a really clear, accessible fashion. As coordinator of student teachers in my school, I will be recommending that the teachers in training that I deal with should have a look at these videos.

Deb (Take Control of the Noisy Class customer)

*   *   *

"I found Rob Plevin's workshop just in time to save me from giving up."

"I found Rob Plevin's workshop just in time to save me from giving up. It should be compulsory – everybody in teaching should attend a Needs-Focused workshop and meet the man with such a big heart who will make you see the important part you can play in the lives of your most difficult students."

Heather Beames (Workshop Attendee)

* * *

"...the ideas, strategies and routines shared with our teachers have led to improved classroom practice."

"The Needs Focused Behaviour Management workshops in support of teacher training in Northern Ireland have been very well received and the ideas, strategies and routines shared with our teachers have led to improved classroom practice. This has been validated by both inspections at the University and observations of teachers."

Celia O'Hagan, (PGCE Course Leader, School of Education, University of Ulster)

* * *

"I have never enjoyed a course, nor learnt as much as I did with Rob."

"What a wonderfully insightful, non-patronising, entertainingly informative day. I have never enjoyed a course, nor learnt as much as I did with Rob. I was so impressed that I am recommending our school invite Rob along to present to all the staff so that we can all benefit from his knowledge, experience and humour."

Richard Lawson-Ellis (Workshop Attendee)

* * *

"...since I started following the principles in your materials, I have seen a vast improvement."

"Hi Rob, I would just like to say that since I started following the principles in your materials, I have seen a vast improvement. I had to teach a one hour interview lesson yesterday and was told that they thought the lesson was super and they loved my enthusiasm! I got the job!

Diane Greene (_Take Control of the Noisy Class customer_)

* * *

"Thanks to you, students from 30 some schools are truly engaged and not throwing pencils at the sub!"

*Rob, Your student engagement series has been out of this world. I've already used various techniques as a substitute and students said I was **the best sub ever.** Thanks to you, students from 30 some schools are truly engaged and not throwing pencils at the sub!"*

Leslie Mueller (Student Engagement Formula customer)

* * *

"So often professional development training is a waste of time; you may get one little gem from a whole day of training. You've given numerous strategies in 5 minutes."

Wow! So many people have gained so much from your videos! Teachers are time poor. A quick grab of effective ideas is what we all need. So often professional development training is a waste of time; you may get one little gem from a whole day of training. You've given numerous strategies in 5 minutes. Thanks for your generosity.

Mary – Ann (Take Control of the Noisy Class customer)

Strategies List